THE COMPLETE POETRY OF JOHN REED

Edited by
Jack Alan Robbins

Introduction by
Granville Hicks

Memoir and Sonnet by
Max Eastman

UNIVERSITY
PRESS OF
AMERICA

Copyright © 1983 by
University Press of America,™ Inc.
P.O. Box 19101, Washington, DC 20036

811
R324c

All rights reserved
Printed in the United States of America

Library of Congress Cataloging in Publication Data

Reed, John, 1887-1920.
  The complete poetry of John Reed.

  Includes bibliography.
  I. Robbins, Jack Alan. II. Title.
PS3535.E2786A17 1983   811'.52   82-21915
ISBN 0-8191-2931-3
ISBN 0-8191-2932-1 (pbk.)

85-0732

TO THE MEMORY OF

DOROTHY AND GRANVILLE HICKS

TABLE OF CONTENTS

Preface - Jack Alan Robbins	ix
Introduction - Granville Hicks	1
Sonnet - To John Reed -- Max Eastman	8

The Complete Poetry of John Reed

Guinevere	11
Tschaikowsky	11
October	12
Aurore	12
The Tempest	13
California	14
The Desert	14
Night	15
The West	15
Coyote Song	16
The Dancing Women	17
The Sea-Gull	17
Origo	18
Horace - Book IV Ode 7	19
Our Lady of Pain	20
John Milton	20
A Winter Run	21
The Sword Dance	22
Dear Heart	23
And Yet -	23
Flowers of Fire	24
The Traveler	24
Forgotten	25
De Profundo	25
Melisande	26
The Chicken	26
Mireille	28
Wanderlust	29
Willamette	30
The Charge of the Political Brigade	31
The Wanderer to His Heart's Desire	32
The Foundations of a Sky-scraper	33
Faery Song	33
Dawn Serenade	34
The First Mate	34
The Slave	35
June in the City	36
The Wedding Ring	36

Valkyrs	37
"This Magazine of Ours"	39
Eleventh Avenue Racket	40
Welsh Song	40
Sangar	41
Tamburlaine	44
A Hymn to Manhattan	45
Deep-Water Song	46
April	47
A Song for May	47
River Side	48
A Farmer's Woman	49
Noon	50
Winter Night	50
A Dedication to Max Eastman	51
Two Rooms	52
Love At Sea	55
Pygmalion	56
Hospital Notes	58
America 1918	59
On Returning to the City	67
Proud New York	68
Fog	68
A Letter to Louise	69
Jack Reed - A Memoir -- Max Eastman	70
The Contributors	81
Acknowledgements	82

Preface

There is no need to retell the story of John Reed's life here, the "Introduction" by Granville Hicks and the "Memoir" by Max Eastman cover that ground in part in quick sketches. The full story can readily be found elsewhere. It is worthwhile, however, to relate the life of John Reed to those of Eastman and Hicks.

Max Eastman was born in Canandaiga in upstate New York, the son of two Congregationalist ministers. His mother, in fact, was the first prominent woman minister in the United States. Max's youth was spent among the villages and farmlands of rural New York. He attended Williams College and went on to study philosophy at Columbia University. While at Columbia Max was taken under the wing of John Dewey, the educator and philosopher of "pragmatism."

During his studies at Columbia, where he received his doctorate in philosophy, Max and his sister Crystal moved into an apartment in Greenwich Village. There in the few years that preceded the First World War Max and Crystal were part of the young bohemian crowd of writers, artists and actors. In 1913 Max and his sister took over the editorial responsibilities of the then floundering radical journal The Masses. It was in the office of The Masses some time later that Max first met John Reed. The latter had graduated Harvard in 1910, had gone to Europe, and was working on the staff of the American Magazine in 1913. Reed had written a short story about a prostitute traveling to Europe and Latin America, and wanted to offer the story to The Masses. From the first reading Max liked the story, although he did not then care much for Reed, who "had a knobby and too filled-out face that reminded me, both in form and color, of a potato. He was dressed up in a smooth brown suit with round pants' legs and a turned-over starched collar, and seemed rather small and rather distracted."* But with time Eastman and Reed grew to be good friends, and Reed was drawn more and more into literary work for The Masses.

---
* Max Eastman, Enjoyment of Living. p. 406

That same year, 1913, Max published his first book, _Enjoyment of Poetry_, an essay on the aesthetics of poetic language and imagery. The book soon became recognized as a classic in its field and is still popular today. Of the more than twenty books Max Eastman did write over a long and fascinating career, _Enjoyment of Poetry_ was clearly his favorite, as he said in a conversation with the editor a few months before his death in March 1969.

Besides their efforts in political journalism for _The Masses_, Eastman and Reed had this great love in common - poetry. Max had begun writing poetry while at Williams; Reed had started even earlier, at Morristown Prep School in New Jersey. Indeed, Reed who was four years younger than Eastman had already written the main body of his poetry by 1913. Both Reed and Eastman brought out slim editions of a few poems, _Sangar_ and _Child of the Amazons_, respectively. Each read and commented on the other's poems.

The year 1913 was quite a formative one for both young writers. For, in addition to their literary activities, Reed and Eastman grew increasingly involved in the struggles of labor. The Paterson (New Jersey) Silk Strike and the Trinidad (Colorado) Miners' Strike were particularly violent, with extreme brutality perpetrated by the government in the defense of the propertied interests against the right of labor to organize and bargain collectively. These and other strikes brought Reed and Eastman into contact with the Wobblies (the I.W.W.), the Socialist Party of Eugene V. Debs, and it was not long before the two had been won over to the banner of revolutionary socialism. Late in the year Reed received journalist credentials to go down to Mexico to cover the Revolution being led there by the "bandit" Pancho Villa, Emiliano Zapata and Venustiano Carranza. Reed went south of the border and even became a friend of Villa, riding with him in the military campaign for Torreon. In Reed's first book completed upon his return to New York, _Insurgent Mexico_, he praised Villa and supported the cause of the Mexican Revolution in vivid prose. He did not encounter Zapata, and Carranza, whom he did meet, did not altogether impress him as did Villa. In 1916 Reed again wrote on Mexico, this time to defend Villa and castigate the Woodrow Wilson Administration for its intervention in Mexican internal affairs.

In August 1914 war broke out in Europe and Reed was not long in waiting to cover some of the action. As a veteran correspondant he represented several New York newspapers and traveled widely throughout Europe, and still sent in editorial pieces to Eastman at The Masses. As socialists Eastman and Reed opposed the war and wanted the earliest possible end of hostilities. The pages of The Masses waged angry polemics to this end, which got the editorial staff in trouble with the Wilson Administration when the U.S. entered the war in April 1917.

Revolution broke out in Russia in March 1917 overthrowing the regime of the Tsar and once again Reed was anxious to be on the scene of the struggle. Eastman set up the contacts and traveling arrangements and Reed journeyed to Petrograd. When Vladimir I. Lenin and Leon Trotsky led the Bolshevik Party to a seizure of power in Petrograd in early November, Reed was on hand and wired reports back to The Masses. Later, these reports were expanded into a book, and the classic eyewitness account of the October (Old Style calendar) Revolution came forth as Ten Days That Shook the World.

Reed returned to the U.S. in 1918 in time for the sedition trial of the editors of The Masses. Eastman, Reed, Art Sloan and the others had been charged with aiding Germany, along with vague imputations of espionage. Dissent on that war was neither popular nor protected, as it was during the Vietnam war. There were two trials that ended in hung juries and the government dropped the charges against the editors. In the meantime The Masses' publication had been suppressed through the machinations of the Post Office Department.

Reed in Petrograd and Eastman in New York were quick to support the cause of the October Revolution and the Soviet leadership of Lenin and Trotsky. On his return to the U.S. Reed served as an emissary for the Bolsheviks to organize an American Communist movement. In 1919 two Communist parties were created: a foreign-language federation-dominated Party which Reed opposed, and an Americanized Communist Labor Party, of which Reed was the founding spirit. Eastman sided with Reed in the clash but neither then nor later did he ever join the Party. Max remained sympathetic but independent, as he never considered himself a Marxist to begin with.

Reed returned to Soviet Russia in 1920 to argue the case for his Communist Labor Party before the Third International. While doing propaganda work for the International in the Caucasus he contracted typhus and died. The available evidence indicates that due to the heavy-handed bureaucratic rule of Zinoviev in the International, Reed had grown rather critical of the Soviet hierarchy and perhaps even of the Bolshevik regime itself. Eastman did not begin to grow distant to the Soviet Union until 1924. Two years earlier he had come for a long visit. While Max was touring the Caucasus himself in early 1924 Lenin had died. Stalin had already maneuvered himself adroitly to prevent Trotsky, then ill, from even attending Lenin's funeral. Max learned of this once back in Moscow. Having earlier befriended Trotsky and being in the process of writing his biography, Max saw the increasing isolation and decline of Trotsky by the triumvirate of Party General Secretary Stalin, International chief Zinoviev, and Moscow Party organization head Kamenev. Throughout the period of the succession struggle, 1924 to 1928, Eastman supported Trotsky, and was the first person to make known the contents of Lenin's "Testament" to the outside world, much to the displeasure of Stalin.

In October 1928 Eastman helped James P. Cannon in launching an American Trotskyist movement, to counterpose the Stalinized Communist Party. During the 1930s Max remained a sympathetic yet independent and critical partisan of Trotsky, refusing to ally himself with the Trotskyist organization. It is quite likely that Max Eastman will continue to be best known as the translator of Trotsky's chief works into English, including the excellent History of the Russian Revolution.

Granville Hicks passed his youth in the New England environment outside of Boston. His father had been a superintendent of a small boiler and radiator factory, and both parents were active in the Unitarian Church. Granville was born in Exeter in 1901. An imaginative and easy-going youth, he was bored with school, but he proceeded through the grades, completing his senior year at Framingham High School in 1919.

Granville went on to Harvard University, as did John Reed before him, although Reed had spent his own youth in the Pacific Northwest. At Harvard Granville studied literature, particularly English literature.

A good deal of his time was devoted to the Universalist Church and to the Young People's Christian Union (YPCU). His literary talents began to emerge when the young Hicks became editor of the YPCU <u>Onward</u>.

The year following graduation Hicks was made literary editor of the <u>Universalist Leader</u>, for which he contributed a weekly column until 1926. During the two years most of the books on Christianity that were published at the time were reviewed in the column. Granville's first book appeared in October 1926, <u>Eight Ways to Look at Christianity</u>, an imaginary eight-way discussion written in the very casual, softly paced and effective manner that would typefy his later narrative style. The structure of the discussion dialogue is, incidentally, strikingly close to that of Andre Malraux's later novel, <u>The Walnut Trees of Altenburg</u>.

In 1928 Granville taught freshman English at Smith College in Northampton, with the future literary biographer and friend Newton Arvin. The following academic year found the youthful Hicks back at Harvard, this time giving an English literature survey course, simultaneously pursuing a Master's degree in literature. Time and the end of the era of prosperity of the 1920s brought Granville more and more away from religious studies and closer to literature.

Rensselaer Polytechnic Institute (R.P.I.) added Granville Hicks to its faculty in 1929. He, his wife Dorothy and young daughter Stephanie moved to the hill country east of Troy, New York, where the Hicks's were to live permanently. That same year Granville was contributing occasional book reviews to the <u>Nation</u> and the <u>New Republic</u>, liberal weekly journals.

By the end of 1931 Hicks had been won over to the Communist movement (although he did not actually join the Communist Party until four years later), as the realities of the Depression became ever more stark. The spiraling unemployment and constant wage cuts throughout the country coupled with the inability of the government to initiate any significant remedy convinced many that the solution must be sought in another kind of political, social and economic system. Marxism appeared to offer the only viable alternative. As Granville much later wrote: "To me and to others like me in the early thirties the teachings of Marx offered both a program for action and a key to the understanding of history. Marx, it seemed to us, had analyzed the origins of capitalism and demonstrated that its internal contradictions would destroy it."*

While Granville proclaimed himself a Marxist in late 1931, he continued to study Marxism with friends and literary acquaintances, and toured the country for various left-wing causes. One product of Granville's intellectual ferment in this period was his study of American literature from the Civil War to the 1930s, The Great Tradition. The first edition appeared in 1933; an updated version to cover the period of "proletarian literature" came out two years later. This book was probably the single most influential work that determined the direction of literary criticism in the middle and late 1930s.

Not long after the stock market crash of 1929 the Communist Party under the leadership of Jay Lovestone and Bertram D. Wolfe created a John Reed Club in New York City. Reed had become a martyr and a legendary figure for the Communists in the decade since his death. The intimations of his disillusionment were known only to a very few - Reed's wife Louise Bryant and his close friend Angelica Balabanoff.⁑ The John Reed Clubs were front organizations to extend Communist influence among young writers. The Clubs did attract many leftward moving writers in the early Depression years. At the beginning of the decade the Lovestone leadership had been expelled from the Communist Party for "Bukharinist deviationism" and was replaced with Earl Browder.

The highpoint of the John Reed Clubs was in the years 1932 to 1935. The Clubs were used to encourage the production of "proletarian literature," the then current literary policy emanating from Moscow. Granville Hicks had joined the John Reed Club of New York in 1933, at first not being very active as he lived considerably far north of Manhattan.

Granville and John Reed had several things in common, having both been Harvard alumni and having been radicalized to the point of joining the Communist movement. The influences that brought Reed over were the violent strikes of the I.W.W. days, the Mexican Revolution, opposition to the First World War

---
* Granville Hicks, The Great Tradition, 1969 Afterword.
⁑ Angelica Balabanoff, My Life As a Rebel, pp. 291-292

and participation in the events of the October Revolution in Russia. Granville had been won over by the reality of the Depression, the rise of Hitler, the Spanish Civil War and the impact of reading Marx's Capital. In temperaments and interests Reed and Hicks were poles apart: Reed was an activist, roving journalist and bohemian; Hicks was more literary, preferring the editorial side of journalism, and stable or settled rather than bohemian in lifestyle. But both shared a deep love for literature and the arts. Reed's Ten Days That Shook the World was one of the books that led Granville to join the Communists.

In the spring of 1934 Corliss Lamont set up a John Reed Committee for Harvard University to call attention to the fact of a radical tradition at Harvard. On the Committee were Roger Baldwin of the Civil Liberties Union, Jack Herling of the Socialist Party, the painter Robert Hallowell, Heywood Broun, Harry Dana, Robert Morss Lovett - and Granville Hicks. The first project was a portrait of John Reed, painted by Hallowell, and presented to the President of Harvard. The second project decided upon was a complete biography of Reed - and Granville welcomed the challenge of writing it.

Granville spent nearly two years researching and writing the life of Reed. The administration of R.P.I. fired him in May 1935 for his radical politics, placing the Hicks family in financial straits for a time. Since January 1934 Granville had been the literary editor of the Communist-controlled journal The New Masses, which attempted to recover the free-wheeling radical spirit of the old Masses of Eastman, Reed and Art Young, - at least as much as was possible within the orthodoxy of Stalinism in its American version. This job and that of manuscript reader for Macmillan sustained the Hicks family after the R.P.I. dismissal.

Before the Reed biography was completed Max Eastman leveled criticism at Granville Hicks in the Modern Monthly. Eastman, then still sympathetic to Trotsky and an ardent critic of the Stalinized Communist Party, believed that as a Communist Hicks would be incapable of writing an unbiased account of Reed's life. For this reason, Max had refused to give any co-operation in the researching of the biography, creating a significant gap in available information.

With the assistance of Reed's widow, Louise Bryant, and researcher John Stuart, Granville finished the biography and Macmillan published it in the fall of 1936. The book, <u>John Reed: The Making of a Revolutionary</u>, was an immediate success and received very favorable reviews, with a few exceptions.

The one major exception was, indeed, Max Eastman, who reviewed <u>John Reed</u> for the <u>Modern Monthly</u>. Max sharply criticized the biography for the portrayal of Reed as a Communist martyr. What Max struck out against was the political implication of the book, rather than the actual merits and accuracy of its contents. His main argument was that the Soviet Russia of the period of 1917 to 1920 under Lenin and Trotsky was a far different country than that under Stalin in the 1930s. The validity of this point would become increasingly clear with the Purge Trials in Moscow of 1936 to 1938 in which Stalin had virtually all of Lenin's old comrades shot. With regard to Granville's book itself, Max disagreed with the emphasis on the political side of Reed's character; he felt that Reed the poet and bohemian was closer to the mark. At any rate, the review by Eastman sparked a violent exchange of views between Reed's friend and his biographer that lasted fully a year.

Somewhat earlier, the Communist Party had dropped the John Reed Clubs by creating in its place an American Writers Conference, following the August 1935 Moscow directive to broaden the Party's popular appeal. The "Third Period" policy of the Communist International of 1928 to 1935 of extreme sectarianism had declared that the Socialists, the Social-Democrats and other leftist and moderate parties were the chief enemy. Instead of focusing its attack on the Fascist threat this policy had only resulted in the isolation of the Communist Party within the working class. This disastrous policy culminated in the rise of Hitler in Germany. By August 1935 Stalin had absorbed the lesson and now ordered a new "Popular Front" policy in which the Communists should ally with anyone seriously intent in combatting Fascism. (It was only at this time that Granville took out actual membership in the Party.) So, the John Reed Clubs and the cult of "proletarian literature" were dropped in favor of more broad-based organizations with the chief theme being opposition to Fascism and war.

Four years later Stalin again reversed policy, when he realized collective security with the Western democracies would not occur, and signed a Nazi-Soviet Non-Aggression Pact and divided up Poland with Germany. The immediate result of this shift was the resignation of Granville Hicks and many others from the American Communist Party. The shadow of war began to reshape the political culture of Europe and America. Finally, in August 1940 Stalin succeeded in having Leon Trotsky murdered in Mexico, and an era stretching from 1917 to 1940 had come to an end, an era in which the Soviet Union could be perceived to be a progressive workers' state, different from other national forms.

On the eve of the fiftieth anniversary of the two Russian Revolutions a new edition of Ten Days That Shook the World was brought out with a new Introduction by Granville Hicks and a resurgence of interest in John Reed developed, in 1967. Most of Reed's writings were reprinted and his example became a model for the young radicals of the Vietnam War generation. With the release of the Warren Beatty motion picture "Reds" in 1981 a renewed interest in Reed developed. Perhaps it may now be said that with this motion picture John Reed has passed from being a legendary figure of the radical Left into acquiring the status of a national hero and symbol of his era. The Granville Hicks edition of Ten Days has been re-issued. Newer and more comprehensive biographical studies of John Reed and Louise Bryant have appeared.

Most of John Reed's poetry was written while he was at Harvard and in the years soon after, before journalistic and political demands consumed so much of his time. Only a handful of poems of the 1915 to 1920 period were ever completed, for his travels as a journalist to Mexico, Europe and Russia did not allow him the opportunity and leisure to finish the many fragments. By any standard the poems that John Reed wrote may not have been literature of the first rank. At the least, however, they were widely read in the periodicals and did influence a number of his contemporaries. Some of the poems were sophomoric, some were parodies, others political, more than a few are quite good. But to Reed the poems were important, for he thought of himself as a poet. And this is how he is now regarded in the general view.

For further reading on John Reed, Max Eastman and Granville Hicks I recommend the following:

William O'Neill, editor, Echoes of Revolt: The Masses 1911-1917. New York: Quadrangle, 1966. 303 pp.

John Stuart, editor, The Education of John Reed. New York: International Publishers, 1955. 271 pp.

Granville Hicks, John Reed: The Making of a Revolutionary. New York: Benjamin Blom, 1968. 445 pp.

.... Part of the Truth. New York: Harcourt, Brace & World, 1965. 314 pp.

.... Where We Came Out. Westport, Conn.: Greenwood Press, 1973. 250 pp.

Jack Alan Robbins, editor, Granville Hicks in the New Masses. Port Washington, N.Y.: Kennikat Press, 1974. 437 pp.

Max Eastman, Enjoyment of Living. New York: Harper, 1948. 600 pp.

.... Love and Revolution. New York: Random House, 1964. 665 pp.

.... Poems of Five Decades. New York: Harper & Row, 1954. 249 pp.

William O'Neill, The Last Romantic: A Life of Max Eastman. New York: Oxford University Press, 1978. 338 pp.

Barbara Gelb, So Short A Time. New York: Berkley Books, 1981. 246 pp.

Robert A. Rosenstone, Romantic Revolutionary. New York: Alfred A. Knopf, 1975. 430 pp.

Floyd Dell, editor, John Reed: Daughter of the Revolution & Other Stories. Freeport, N.Y.: Books for Libraries Press, 1970. 164 pp.

Daniel Aaron, Writers on the Left. New York: Avon Books, 1961. 480 pp.

Books quoted above:

Granville Hicks, _The Great Tradition_. New York: Quadrangle Books, 1969. New Afterword by author.

Angelica Balabanoff, _My Life As a Rebel_. New York: Harper & Row, 1938.

INTRODUCTION

Granville Hicks

John Reed, who died in Moscow on October 17, 1920, five days before his thirty-third birthday, has been remembered all these years because of a book, *Ten Days That Shook the World*, and because of his martyrdom. He went to Russia in the early autumn of 1917, and out of his observations and research came *Ten Days*, which, half a century after the Bolshevik Revolution, is generally regarded as an authoritative description and interpretation of that event. But Reed was not one to be content with the writing of history; he came home to help organize what eventually became the Communist Party of the United States of America, and he returned to Russia to attend the congress of the Third International. Although he had been weakened by weeks spent in a Finnish prison, he went to Baku to participate in a Congress of Oriental Nations, and it was on the way back to Moscow that he was smitten with typhus.

But there is more to Reed's story than that, nor is *Ten Days* his only memorable book. In 1914 he published *Insurgent Mexico*, made up of articles he had written for the *Metropolitan Magazine*. Even more strikingly than *Ten Days*, this book exhibits Reed's gifts as a reporter. It is a piece of brilliantly vivid writing, but it also has interest as an examination of one phase of a complicated and long-continuing revolutionary movement.

John Silas Reed was born in Portland, Oregon, in 1887. His father, who was known as a wit up and down the Pacific Coast, had crossed the continent as the representative of manufacturers of mowers and reapers. He was a successful business man but not a conventional one, and later on he supported Theodore Roosevelt in his anti-trust campaign, serving for a time as United States Marshal. Reed's mother, on the other hand, was proud of belonging to one of Portland's best families, the Greens, and accepted all the proper ideas of her class.

Jack Reed was educated in the East, first at Morristown School in New Jersey, then at Harvard College. In his early youth he was shy and rather unwell, but at Morristown he emerged as a versatile leader - an editor of the school monthly, a member and manager of the football team, and the first boy to be suspected when there was mischief afoot. Harvard was a different matter. Reed was not good enough for the football team, and being cheerleader, though fun, was a poor substitute. He did excel in swimming, and was captain of the water polo team, but these were minor sports. Nor was he satisfied by his literary successes, although he was elected to the staff of the <u>Harvard Monthly</u> and was Ibis (#2 man) on the <u>Lampoon</u>. Except for an indifference to grades, he wanted to excel in every department of undergraduate life, and it was a source of grief to him that he was not chosen by any of the socially exclusive clubs. He had many friends, but the proper Harvard men tended to regard him as a bounder.

The only member of the Harvard faculty who had an important influence on Reed was Charles Townsend Copeland - "Copey," Harvard faculty's only eccentric and, as it may have seemed to Reed, almost its only human being. Reed acknowledged his debt by dedicating <u>Insurgent Mexico</u> to Copey: "As I wrote these impressions of Mexico I couldn't help but think that I never would have seen what I did see if it had not been for your teaching me. I can only add my word to what so many who are writing have already told you: That to listen to you is to learn how to see the hidden beauty of the visible world, that to be your friend is to try to be intellectually honest."

A more important influence was non-academic: Lincoln Steffens, who was a friend of Reed's father, promised him that Jack would have his chance to make a start in the literary world. So, when Reed returned from a romantic summer in Europe after graduation from Harvard, Steffens got him a job on the <u>American Magazine</u>. It was a routine job, Steffens said, but it would help Jack to find himself. Reed took rooms in an old house on Washington Square, in which several of his college friends were living. Steffens had a room here when he was in town, and Reed showed him what he wrote and listened to his criticism. Steffens made no effort to convert Reed to his own more or less radical point of view, but encouraged him to use his eyes and to treat words with respect.

These were the exuberant years. John Dos Passos labeled his sketch of Reed in U.S.A. "Playboy": "Reed was a man; he liked men he liked women he liked eating and drinking and foggy nights and drinking and foggy nights and swimming and football and rhymed verse and being cheerleader ivy orator making clubs (not the best clubs, his blood did not run thin enough for the very best clubs)." In some ways Reed was a playboy: he loved adventure, was full of boisterous good humor, took pleasure in shocking the bourgeois. But the word has come to mean something else - wealth, self-indulgence, extravagant idleness. In that sense Reed was not a playboy. He would have been amused by going to a Playboy Club, but once would have been enough. He was a worker. He wanted to be a writer, and he was prepared to discipline himself in the craft. He did an amusing poem about his friends in the Village, "The Day in Bohemia," and he wrote a lively satire for presentation by the Dutch Treat Club, Everymagazine. This sort of thing was fun, but Reed was a craftsman even when he was trying to make people laugh, and at the same time he was writing serious poems. He had begun to write poetry as a student at Morristown, and had continued at Harvard, but his best poems were written during the playboy years, 1910 to 1913, and they were not the work of a playboy, as this collection will show.

Gradually Reed was learning that life wasn't all fun. A magazine, The Masses, had been founded in 1911 by a man named Piet Vlag, as an expression of both Bohemian rebelliousness and political revolt. Late in 1912 the staff was reorganized, and Max Eastman became editor. A few months later Reed joined the staff - this was not, of course, a paying job - and began to contribute sketches of life in New York of a sort that the American and the other slick magazines would not touch. In drafting a statement of purpose for The Masses, he wrote that the editors would publish what they pleased: "We have perfect faith that there exists in America a wide public, alert, alive, bored with the smug procession of magazine platitudes, to whom What We Please will be a fresh wind..... Poems, stories, and drawings rejected by the capitalistic press will find a welcome in the magazine." The Masses became a wonderfully lively magazine, for there was a chaotic spirit of revolt boiling up in America. Such artists as Art Young, Maurice Becker, and John Sloan, and such writers as Max Eastman, Arturo Giovannitti, Harry Kemp, and John Reed expressed that spirit in The Masses.

Reed was beginning his political education. Lincoln Steffens kept asking questions that made him look below the surface of things. Attending Mabel Dodge's salon at 23 Fifth Avenue, Reed met and listened to such radicals as Hutchins Hapgood, Emma Goldman, and Big Bill Haywood of the I.W.W. One evening Haywood talked about the strike of the silk workers in Paterson, and the next day Reed went to see for himself. Ordered by a police officer to move, he stood on his rights and was arrested. During the four days he spent in jail he talked with Carlo Tresca, a fiery Italian strike leader, who stirred Reed with his stories of the miseries of the strikers. After his release, Reed spent much of his time speaking on behalf of the strikers and raising money to help them. From somewhere came the idea of staging a pageant in Madison Square Garden, and Reed not only threw his own vast energies into the project but commandeered the support of his friends. The pageant was a great success as a piece of propaganda and a complete financial failure.

In one of her autobiographical volumes, Movers and Shakers, Mabel Dodge Luhan has written that it was she who suggested the pageant and inspired Reed in his labors. ("I knew I was enabling Reed to do what he was doing," she wrote. "I knew he couldn't have done it without me.") However that may be, she swept him off to Italy once the pageant had been produced, and for a time they were lovers.

Upon his return in October, he became managing editor of the Masses, and did considerable writing for the magazine. He was by now a strong supporter of the cause of the workers, but he was loath to commit himself to the Socialist Party or the I.W.W. or any other organization, not because he was afraid of the practical consequences but because any commitment seemed bound to narrow the range of his activities. It was at this time of decision that the Metropolitan Magazine, on the suggestion of Lincoln Steffens, sent Reed to Mexico to report on the revolution that was taking place there. The Metropolitan, under the editorship of Carl Hovey, had begun to publish work by such leftists as Morris Hillquit, Lincoln Steffens,

Israel Zangwill, and Bernard Shaw. Because the magazine was subsidized by a millionaire sportsman, Harry Payne Whitney, the radicals did not take it very seriously, but it gave them a hearing and money to boot. Steffens was certain that Reed would do a great job, and of course he did.

The Mexican assignment enabled Reed to postpone the problem of his future and gave him some of the most stimulating experiences of his life. Villa had taken Chihuahua City, and it was there that Reed joined him near the end of 1913. He interviewed the rebel leader, and soon they were friends. He witnessed the battle of Torreon, risking his life to watch the successive stages of the attack. He lived with Villa's soldiers, drank with them, gambled with them, danced with their women. He made friends and saw them killed in battle. He identified himself so completely with Villa's army that he told friends he would join it if the United States invaded Mexico.

This was a romantic revolution, and the articles Reed wrote about it were full of color and full of the excitement and joy he was feeling. But there was intellectual as well as emotional involvement. It seemed clear to Reed that Villa represented the peons, who made up nine-tenths of Mexico's population, and that intervention by the United States would result in the strengthening of the aristocratic landowners. Reed loved Mexico, even its filth and bloodshed, because the Mexicans were unstandardized, warm-hearted, irresponsible. Romance, unconventionality, and justice were all on one side, the happiest combination Reed could imagine. As for Villa, he seemed sincere, the people loved him, he was infinitely courageous, and he was willing to learn. On his return to the States, Reed wrote letters and articles against intervention, and he sought for and was given an appointment with President Wilson, to whom he presented his views on Villa.

As a result of the articles on Mexico, Reed was hailed as one of the great war correspondents, and it was inevitable that he should be sent to France when World War I began. In the meantime he had done a stunning article on another kind of war - the class war in Ludlow, Colorado. Ten days before he reached Ludlow, four hundred militiamen, detectives, and strikebreakers had marched upon the striking miners' tent colony with bombs and machine guns. Joined by other militiamen, they had soaked the tents with kerosene and set them on fire, and then shot at the women and children as they ran from the flames. Captured strike-leaders were murdered. Scores of men, women and children were killed; from the cellar hole of a single tent charred bodies of thirteen women and children were afterwards taken. Having surveyed the scene and talked with survivors, Reed studied the records of the three major coal companies, the Congressional testimony of John D. Rockefeller, Jr., and the reports of the State Commissioner of Labor. Out of his own muckraking experience, Steffens had taught Reed the importance of documentation, and Reed was an apt pupil.

The war in Europe was very different from the war in Mexico - terribly destructive and deadly dull. This, as Reed saw it, was the systematic slaughter of innocent men, driven to their deaths by organized pressure exerted in every fashion that the ruling classes could devise. He came home with a single message, "This is not our war". Nor was his mind changed by what he saw a little later on the Eastern Front.

In 1915 and 1916 he could still write articles for the Metropolitan and other popular magazines so long as he did not express his views on the war. So he wrote about the political conventions and Bryan and Billy Sunday for Collier's and the Metropolitan, and said what he thought it really important to say in the Masses. It was in this period that he met and married Louise Bryant, and during the summer of 1916 he and she took part in the founding of the Provincetown Players. But as the United States drew closer to war with Germany, his opposition became stronger and stronger, and he spoke frequently at anti-war meetings. Once war had been declared, the popular magazines dropped him, and he found himself writing for the New York Mail, which, it was later revealed, was being financed by the German government. (Reed did not know this, but I am not sure he would have minded so long as he was allowed to tell what he believed to be the truth.)

When the Czar of Russia was overthrown in the spring of 1917, Reed had a passionate desire to see what was happening; but the slick magazines, whose

editors had been fighting to secure his services a
little more than a year earlier, would not touch him.
His trip to Russia was financed by friends, and his
only credentials came from the Masses, the Socialist
Call, and the Seven Arts. He arrived in time to analyze
the weaknesses of the Kerensky administration and
to observe the growing power of the Bolsheviks. When
the overthrow of the provisional government began,
he knew exactly what was happening. The poet in him,
the journalist, the student and the socialist fused in
one dynamic and indefatigable person. He tried to see
everything that was happening, and at the same time he
collected the proclamations, manifestos, decrees, and
resolutions that all the parties and factions were
wildly issuing. When he reached New York on April 28,
1918 - exactly five years after his arrest in Paterson
his papers were confiscated, and they were not re-
leased until the end of the year. Then, hiding himself
from his comrades and friends in a rented room in
Greenwich Village, he wrote Ten Days in less than ten
weeks.

On November 17, 1917, he had written to the
Masses: "For the first time in history the working
class has seized the power of the state for its own
purposes - and means to keep it. So far as anyone
can see, there is no force in Russia to challenge the
Bolshevik power. And yet, as I write this, in the
flush of their success, the new-born revolution of the
proletariat is ringed round with a vast fear and hatred.
The proletarian revolution has no friends except the
proletariat." (Before the dispatch could reach New
York, the Masses had been suppressed and the editors,
including Reed, had been charged with conspiring "to
obstruct recruiting and enlistment to the injury of
the service".) Reed knew that his duty now was to
tell the workers of the world, and specifically the
workers of the United States, what had happened in
Russia and to persuade them to follow the example of
the Bolsheviks. To these ends he devoted the short
remainder of his life.

Grafton, New York

To John Reed

by MAX EASTMAN

Jack, you are quiet now among the dead.
The pulse of the young lion and the fire
In that bright engine of extreme desire
That never would be tired or quieted,
That could fight, laugh, give, love, and sing,
And understand, so carelessly - so strong
That you amazed us with your tender song -
It all is dead now, dead and mouldering.

They say you died for communism - they
Who to some absent god must always give
The choicest even of the fruits of youth.
Your god was life. Because you chose to live,
Death found you in the torrent of the fray,
Exulting in the future and the truth.

THE

COMPLETE POETRY

OF

JOHN REED

THE

COMPLETE POETRY

OF

JOHN REED

Guinevere

A thousand years ago we two were young
And dwelt in that gray castle by the sea,
Whose sombre surges swayed eternally
The dreary rhythm of some forgotten song;
And nothing lived nor moved the whole day long
Save you and I; and through our ceaseless tears
We saw the vista of those tragic years,
And godlike Arthur's soul with passion wrung.

List to the awful kingly dirge; the sea
Pours out his grieving heart with anguished wail
Against the gray deserted cliffs, the while
A dazzling presence shows its light to me;
I, blinded, whisper, "Art thou, then, the Grail?"
And "Nay" it answers, "but the sad queen's smile."

Harvard Monthly
July 1907

Tschaikowsky

Awake! Ye people of the North, arise!
Tschaikowsky calls you from his mountain height
And, godlike, shakes his splendid spear of light
Athwart the harp-strings of the sounding skies.
List to the anthem; hearts and souls afire,
The people march, and singing breast the steep
Invincible, a tide upon the deep,
Storm-driven by his eagle-wingèd lyre.
No looking back, no mourning in the past,
But stern and brave the music sweeps along,
Content to die, if this hour be the last,
A river of imperishable song.
O new Prometheus, spread your stolen fire
And break the chains of darkness and of wrong!

Harvard Monthly
October 1907

October

Languorous with heavy haze
   Sinks the scarlet sun. A drowsy hush
Hangs above the city ways
   And stills their rush.

Smoky mist of forest fires
   Greyly palls the distance. Pines long dead
Smolder deep like dead desires
   Their gaunt arms spread.

Golden-Red the honeyed moon
   Swarmed about with golden bees, hangs low
Climbing to her silver noon
   With blood-like glow.

Weirdly floats the echo down
   Tom-Toms faintly throbbing far away
Through the mist from Chinatown
   Across the bay.

Pacific Monthly
October 1907

Aurore

Now in the East pale sleeping fairies weave
From dreams the wan grey gossameer of dawn
And lay it on your hair, so fair, so fair.
You sleep - and yet the shadowy dancers leave.

The swaying phantoms one by one are gone.
The deathless music fades in breathless air.
Come, all the earth is singing to the sky
Touch with your eyes the tapers of the world.

Day rises from the arms of night - star spun.
White roses lift against your balcony, strange
   flower-fire.
The lark with song unfurl'd soars up,
To beat his wings against the sun.

(Unpolished poem written at 4 a.m. on January 1, 1908.)

The Tempest

As Pallas sprang from the head of Zeus,
    Divine in her splendid mail,
I leapt full-armed from the Sun-god's brow
    And rode on the roaring gale.
A thousand leagues to the east we fled,
    While heaven and earth and sea
Arose to the tread of my mighty feet
    In terrible symphony.
I sang of wars in the dawn of time,
    Of worlds in the outer night,
I stabbed the dark with my two-edged sword,
    And struck in a burst of light.
The great ship drove on the rocks aflame,
    A towering funeral pyre,
While I swooped down on the chattered coast
    And tortured the land with fire.

    . . . .

But lo! the heart of the mystic east
    Is drawing the veil away,
I weaken, bound in a drowsy charm,
    The spell of another day.
My father comes; with a slower pace,
    I languidly seek my rest.
And deep in the poppied warmth I sink
    Asleep on the Sun-god's breast.

Harvard Monthly
January 1908

California

These many years the hoary missions lie
Under the turquiose sky
Smiling, like white-haired priests asleep,
Who dream of happy memories.
And still the blue Sierras keep
Their ancient guard above the flow'ring orange trees.
When softly, like a dusky cowl,
The odorous night wraps round the day,
And in the purple deep
The dying sun is laid away,
His only requiem a mournful owl,
Alone, and owl-like, mourning unremembered wrong.
Then rings the ghostly Angelus so sweet
That, shattered by a song,
The years turn back to Spanish nights
Two hundred years ago; and from the street
The mellow twang of the guitar
Some dark-eyed belle invites
Out into the star-gardens of the sky
And passes in the distance down the road
From Santa Barbara to Mirimar.

Harvard Monthly

February 1908

The Desert

That solemn waste is hushed forevermore
And nothing lives, but on the desert sand
Lost souls trace with imperishable hand
The secrets of their mystic, deathly lore.
Like ruins of some vast Titanic war
The shattered desert lies, nor wakes the land
Save in the storm, when at the god's command
The mailed lightning shakes the rocky floor.
All night the caravans of stars go by
In silence. Still the sombre waste-land keeps
Its lonely watch while all the heaven sleeps,
And the lone moon is drowsy in the sky.
How delicate the trembling thrill that leaps
From heart to heart, as the pale star-fires die!

Harvard Monthly

April 1908

Night

I.

Tonight the surf gleams with a thousand fires,
Lost fragments of an ancient moon
That fell into the sea long, long ago,
Down through a night of some forgotten June.

II.

Just a lone sea-bird crying in the dark,
While sea and sky their vigil keep,
With solemn litany of wind and surge
Deep calling unto everlasting deep.

Pacific Monthly
May 1908

The West

Gulls to their home on the aged rock
    Wheeling athwart the spray,
Thrill of the wind from the isles of Ind
    In the heart of the dying day.

Dreams in the depths of the solemn pines
    Ancient before our birth,
Hearing the speech of the plains that reach
    To the ends of the happy earth.

Out of the years that have passed away
    Out of the days to be,
Night brings the pang of the salt air's tang
    And the call of the West to me.

Harvard Advocate
June 15, 1908

Coyote Song

A - oo, my brothers, the moon is red,
And the antelope starts from his prairie bed,
Then join ye again in the ancient threne,
    For the day that's dead,
    And the hunt that's fled,
And the terror of things unseen.

Afar, afar, on the star-lit plain,
Our fathers howled where the deer had lain,
And hung on the flanks of the bison-run,
    For the bull that fell,
    In that wild pell-mell,
Had died ere the night was done.

No more the warrior rides his raids,
And the hunting star of the prairie fades,
While a fiery comet tears the night
    With a crimson streak
    And a demon's shriek,
All ablaze with the white man's light.

But oft when the winter wind is high,
We hear on the prairie the bellowed cry
And the rumbling hoofs of the bison-run.
    But we seek in vain,
    Through the empty plain,
For the buffalo days are done.

A - oo, my brothers, the stars are red
And the lean coyote must mourn unfed.
Come join ye again in the ancient croon,
    For the dawn is gray,
    And another day
Has faded the red, red moon.

Harvard Monthly
October 1908

The Dancing Women

Who never see the Light of Life,
    Because their tortured spirits sleep,
Who drift beyond the shallow bar
    And out upon the reckless deep,
Are half the grief of this fair world
    That makes the weary angels weep.

Gray ashes on the hearth of God,
    Forever scattered by His breath,
See how they dance along a wind
    Thronged with the shapeless forms of death,
The garish lights their beacon fire,
    The blasphemy their shibboleth.

Harvard Monthly
October 1908

The Sea-Gull

Wet with the stinging spray he skims the deep,
A livid gleam of life, and scans afar
Where the great breakers pound across the bar,
Beneath the headlands where his nestlings sleep.
Above the light the keeper sees him sweep
From fog to fog, and vanish like a star
Down where the unknown ocean monsters are,
And hears his mournful crying on the steep.

And when on winter days he rises high
Against the squall, and swift on-coming night,
And bares his gleaming armor to the fight,
Then are the sailors startled by his cry;
Darting spear-like athwart the dark'ning main
To ride the helmet of the hurricane.

Harvard Advocate
October 16, 1908

Origo

This - with the sigh of the dark sad trees that stand
Aloft on yon battlement, looking across the land,
Rooted age-deep in the crumbling canyon rock,
Suffering, fog-wreathed, the sea-driven tempest's shock.
This - where the gloomy walls of the river's bed
Climb toward the forest murmuring overhead,
Learning the song on the soft Chinook that bears
Smiles for the fruitful land, for the arid, tears;
With the luminous moon so soft behind the mist
And a thin sweet star that a spruce's tuft has kissed.

I seem the first to have seen this, I the last
I the only one, yet in ages past
Who knows but some Indian, treading at dusk the wood
Paused on the edge of the bluff, and listening, stood
Then just as I, with a shower of crumbling clay,
Half climbed, half slipped to the bottom where twilight
    grey
Already was veiling the wondrous face of Day.
Long time he stood, and the roar of the upper fall
Beat in his ears. From the top of the canyon wall
A black hawk lifted and sailing across the sky
Portended evil, harshly sounding his cry.

Then gazing about him, waded the icy stream
Where the dim cliffs like misty phantoms seem
Ghosts from the realm of some forgotten dream.
And, as the demon darkness swallowed the light
Donning his starry armor diamond-bright.
The firelight touched the Indian's swarthy face
As he crooned some song of his mystic savage race.
And the moon peeped down from the feathered cloud
    she rode
Where a silver stream through a silver canyon flowed.

Then Dawn was born, and with the coming light
The Eagle Sun soared from the realm of night.
Then roused himself the Indian, sprang far out
Into a shadowed pool and threshed about
With tawny limbs. Emerged with body bare
And shook the water from his shining hair.
Then, dripping crystal drops, he climbed the wall
And, standing like a gleaming statue tall
Against the forest green he gazed once more
Down where the living water chafed its shore

The silver trout that leaped from out the stream
And the murmur like the whisper of a dream
Long-past and half-forgotten, soft and sweet
The patter of innumerable feet
Adorn the twilight of Eternity.
He turned, and soundless, vanished.

Unpublished - 1908

Horace - Book IV Ode 7

All fled are the snows; now the meadows and forests
    awaken
Clotted in their beautiful hair
The land thrills anew with the change and the rivers
    subsiding
Flow with a languider air.

Again in the moonlight the grace intertwined with her
    sisters
Sways in the passionate dance
"Hope not for Eternity" saying, the year and the moment
Hasten the bright day's advance.

All night the swift moons in the heavens renew their
    lost brilliance
Yet when we go to our doom
Where Tullens has gone, and Aeneas our father, and Ancus
We are but dust of the tomb.

Who knows if the high gods will crown with another
    tomorrow
This summer sky of today?
Be happy then, living, for riches, once you have departed
Heirs will but lavish away.

When once you have fallen, Torquatus, and over your
    spirit
Minos has given decree
Then not all your goodness, nor treasure, nor silver-
    tongued pleading
Ever can bring you to me.

Our Lady of Pain

Brown waffles and mellow molasses
Welsh rarebit that bites us and burns
Budweiser that fills up our glasses
The waiter that turns and returns
When these have gone by with their glories
What then to our stomachs remain?
Thou! Mystic and savage Dolores
Our Lady of Pain!

We physic and doctor and dope us
Thou art smoking and tempting and hot
What matter if pains telescope us
We eat thee, dyspepsia or not
Nor health nor hygiene is the question
So fill up the bumpers again
Thou wilt come when we have indigestion
Our Lady of Pain!

1908-1909?

John Milton

Apollo! Master of the deep-toned lyre
Still burns your altar-fire
Above the worshippers; still silver-browed
They breathe the flame:
He of the immortal name
Who faced the dread of utter sleep unbowed
He that aroused the soul to swift alarms
And the high thrill of arms
And the fair spirit in whose lyric voice
The winds and birds are mingled - "Ah rejoice
For all the earth is singing to the sky - "
In ecstasy
They seek to follow where your sandals trod -
Yet vain
The struggle and the pain
They are but mortal men and you - a god.

Ere morning touched the tapers of the world
You were abroad. The orient day
Broke in a thousand splendours on your way:
And where the raving breakers swirled
Across the bar, you heard the ocean speak
To God in the bushed paleness of the dawn.

Or in the moonlight, watched the laughing form
Dance with the motley fairies; or would seek
Some lovely spot, and pierce beyond the stars
With sure unhampered vision that saw
The dread avengers of the changeless Saul
And splendid Satan beating at the bars.
To them that dream, you stand
Above the altar; rapt unseeing eyes
Rending the awful veil of Paradise
Impassioned hand
Sweeping the trembling strings: far hurled
The music sweeps across the sky
In one majestic symphony
The mingled tears and laughter of the world.

1908-1909?

A Winter Run

Out of the warmth and the light,
    Into the frosty weather,
Into the teeth of a winter's night,
    Running, we sprang together.

The icy, silent dark leapt up
    And struck me in the face —
And the moon hung out her silver cup
    As trophy for the race.

Our driving breath flung out behind
    Like some dim, flying plume;
Our shadows, on the snow outlined,
    Ran with us in the gloom.

The long white road, the rhythmic beat,
    The wind-sword in our hair —
On, here's the spell of winged feet,
    The charm of winter air!

A flashing glimpse, a scarce-seen face,
    A figure clear, then gone,
Once more the dark, the swinging pace,
    And on again, and on.

Across the river dim and still
    The heedless sleepers lie,
And, finger-like, the towered hill
    Stands up against the sky.

Into the warmth and the light,
    Out of the frosty weather,
Out of the chill of a winter's night,
    Glowing, we sprang together.

Harvard Illustrated Magazine
January 1909

The Sword Dance

Clash! Clash! Sing, old sword!
Sing the skirling pipes of battle!
Once again the gleaming Forgail,
Red-haired, passion-throated, shouting,
Leads his clan in reeling combat.
Clash! Clash! Sing, old sword!

Clash! Clash! We are old.
Down the red-mailed sky at evening
Floats the dust of warrior princes;
Down the steel-clad sky at evening
Swings the battle-chant of Forgail.
Clash! Clash! We are old.

Harvard Monthly
February 1909

Dear Heart

Dear Heart, pale stars through the quiet night
Swing with a languorous music across the deep
And bring a wonderful peace to the hearts of men.

And you, so wan, from your fearful fight,
Throb still with the pain of your thinking. The angel Sleep
Wings softly, bearing you back to the skies again.

I see you smile in the silver light,
Sleeping, a child again, whispering tremulous words
To nameless souls in the child-world beyond our ken.

Harvard Monthly

March 1909

And Yet -

Here do we part, you and the rest to stay
   In the red valley where the lotus weaves
Glad pain with sleep; and up the rugged way.
   I go alone, and wish I might forget.
   And yet - and yet -

The sun is on the upland sheaves,
And all the grass with starry tears is wet.

Work! Work! Something to dull the ache
   Of petty friends and little souls - ah, vain,
All vain the grief that you and you awake.
   Gone is the old unutterable thrill,
   and still - and still -

I hear from our the driving wraiths of rain
The brown thrush singing on the upland hill.

Harvard Monthly

March 1909

Flowers of Fire
(adapted from the French of Heredia)

For ages since the first chaotic night
   Flame lifted from this crater toward the sky,
   And red plumes, since the dawn of memory,
Waved over Chimborazo's lonely height.
No echo stirs the silence of the peak;
   Where ashes rained, a solitary bird
   Drinks from the rain-pools; and the earth interred
Beneath its lava-blood, is sere and bleak.

Sometimes, last effort of the ancient fire,
   The lava-bubbles, cold with ancient years,
     Burst with sound of thunder in the hills;
And like the flare of some great funeral-pyre,
   Amid gray rocks and yellow dust uprears
     The crimson cactus, red with earth-fire still.

Harvard Monthly
May 1909

The Traveler

He sailed from Egypt under pleasant skies
   Proud of his ship, and gazing toward the South
   Where Pharos faded at the harbor-mouth,
Nor did he heed Arcturus on the rise.
No more he'll see the Alexandrine mole;
   But in the barren sand of some far shore,
   Where one lone tree is wind-tossed ever more,
The storm has carved a chamber for his soul.

Laid in the deepest hollow of the dune
   The traveler has found his rest at last,
     Forever wrapped in starless, dreamless night.
So still he lies beneath the Grecian moon . . .
   Above his body, whence the fire has passed.
     O Sea, be silent, and, O Earth, be light.

Harvard Monthly
May 1909

Forgotten
(adapted from the French of Heredia)

The temple falls to ruin on the cape,
And utter sleep has mingled with the mold
The marble gods and paladins of old, -
Locked in the prison whence is no escape.
Sometimes the lonely herdsman drives his kine
To the clear lake, and wakes the ancient pain,
With the sad piping of an old refrain, -
Clear-cut against the far horizon-line;
The kindly Earth guards well its old regime
And each Spring, vainly eloquent, doth dower
The broken pillar with a new-born flower:
But man, unheedful of his father's dream,
Fears not to hear each night, unchangingly,
The vast, eternal sorrow of the sea.

Harvard Monthly
May 1909

De Profundo

Up from the deep! Oh God - if God there be,
    so must I spring - hand in each wretched hand
    heart to dead heart of these that wear the brand -
    the reckless, sightless drift of destiny.
Flesh of the nameless drunkard of the street,
    blood of his blood who lives the low and vile,
    lover of her who, for a little while
    forgets, seared with the terrible and sweet.

Oh bitter bitter must he drink to taste
    The immortal - must be blind to see the light -
    human with human sin, ere deified.
Thus only may I pass the dreary waste,
    leap to the unimaginable height,
    and tread the star-trails where the Valkyrs ride!

Harvard Monthly
October 1909

Melisande

Ah, white, still sister of the blossom-fire,
your lips again! Across the twilight world
the driving wraiths of mist are hurled,
to shroud us in alone with our desire.

Torn by the silver talons of the rain
the wounded petals cover you, - less fair
than the wild fragrance of your hair,
less sweet than this sweet ecstacy of pain.

White maid, there is no God but the red flame
that burns so fiercely in your breast - no bliss
but the hot passion of your kiss -
no music but the whisper of your name.

Harvard Monthly

November 1909

The Chicken
(with apologies to the shadow of Poe)

I

Once upon a midnight dreary, as I chuckled weak and
    weary
Over many a saintly "Spinster" and unsaintly "Troubadour"
While I chortled nearly splitting, suddenly there came
    hitting
As of someone gently kicking, biffing at my chamber
    door,
Only that and nothing more.

II

And the rustling of the stitches on my Sunday pair of
    britches
Thrilled me - filled me with fantastic terrors never
    felt before.
So my faint heart to be quelling, I stood up while
    loudly yelling
"Hurry up, come in, you idiots, and be sure to close
    the door"
Silence there and nothing more.

III

Presently my wrath grew stronger; hesitating then no
   longer,
I walked over to the threshold and threw wide my
   chamber door
Deep into the darkness peering, long I stood there,
   wondering, fearing,
Hearing muchly to be smitten with a rotten apple core.
Merely this and nothing more.

IV

Back into my chamber turning, all my heart within me
   burning
Soon again I hear the biffing, somewhat louder than
   before
"Surely" said I "surely that is eggs against my window
   lattice
For it soundeth like the shoes of Brother Mike upon
   the floor.
That it is and nothing more."

V

Open wide I flung the shutter, when, with many a flirt
   and flutter,
In there stepped a stately chicken of the saintly days
   of yore
Not the least obeisance made she; not an instant
   stopped or stayed she.
Perching on the bust of Bill Nye just above my chamber
   door,
Laid an egg upon the floor.

VI

Then methought the air grew denser, perfumed from an
   unseen censer,
Swung by editors whose footsteps tinkled in the
   corridor.
"Wretch" I cried "A spirit lent thee - but to haunt
   we here he sent thee.
Get thee hence, and never darken with thy wing my
   chamber door!"
Quoth the chicken "Nevermore."

VII

"Prophet" said I "Thing of evil! - prophet still, if
   hen or devil,
Tell me, will Ol' Herriott ever get a read-nuttance
   more?
Will Fourteenth Street gate be cut through, and the
   happy children butt through?
And won't they have to go around the long way as
   before?"
Crowed the chicken, "Nevermore!"

VIII

"Be that word our sign of parting, bird or fiend,"
   I shrieked, upstarting
"Take thy feet from off my Bill Nye and thy eggs
   from off my door!"
But the chicken never flitting, on my Bill Nye still
   is sitting,
And the egg that lies within the shadow floating on
   the floor
Shall be lifted - Nevermore!

Editor's Note: This is a parody of Edgar Allen Poe's
well-known poem "The Raven". Reed wrote the parody
while at Harvard in 1909 and signed it "Edgar Allen
Reed".

Mireille

Mireille! O every heart wherein there stirs
Free wind of wide lands, clangor of old bells
Savour of mystical and fragrant tales
Mourns for Mireille. The silent worshipper
At sunset, inarticulate, who swells
With an ethereal voiceless breath the sails
Of far-away barquetos - thus am I
Mireille! Before thy history.

Out of a world of smoky belching fires
That foul the blue sky of the world - away
From the dull scream of might engines, and
The crash of iron cities, - hot desires

Of starving souls that knew thee not, Mireille -
From cynic heart and bitter word and hand
You breathe a half-heard song of old Provence
Mireille! Fresh minstrel of Romance.

I too know Avignon the mighty-walled
Have mused at dusk in cloistered St. Trophime
And roamed at night Beaucaire and Tarascon
With the old Trouveres, when the eucre called;
On Mont Major and Baux made feast in dream
With Rene and the warriors long agone
And kissed the Rano Jano's white white hand
Mireille! In your enchanted land.

O Sun Provencal, flaming with the stark
Pure fire of spirits of dead poets, high
In sapphire o'er the vast Camargue, wide-spread,
Your gory death-cloths hand - while the slow dark
Creeps up the East; when does the soul descry
Seaward the faint far country of the dead -
O Sun, thus die with every tragic day
For you have stricken fair Mireille.

O southern Moon! Who rests so lovingly
Each night, a thousand years, on ruined things -
Pale splendour lumined with dead virgin's breath
Touching with radiance mas and low airee
And the dim jasmine where the motteu sings -
Who wakes old castles garrisoned with Death
Weep Moon! and loosen tresses of star-fire
You led Mireille to her desire.

1910?

Wanderlust

By the trackless shore of the sea, where the alien
    shouting of breakers
  Beats on a desolate land, and is lost in the swirl
    of the dunes, -
The unsatisfied souls of the sea-dead wander the
    flowerless acres,
  Tracing in shadowless sand their mystic ineffable
    runes.
For the sea calls to go forth to the sea and the
    world's far ending,

And the gull's cry carries the sound of gongs from
    the temples of Ind,
And the phantoms of wanderers suffer from lust and
    desire unending,
  Luring with scent of strange flowers caught in the
    hair of the wind,
O call of our Mother and Bride, fierce Earth that
    entices with danger,
  Whose kiss is a Pain and a Torture, whose passion
    is ultimate Death!
I follow thee Eastward alone, with a love that is
    wilder and stranger
  Than that of the dead who have mingled their breath
    with the flame of thy breath.
The wrath of the sea is thy robe, and thy breasts are
    the measureless mountains,
  And the fire of thy spirit burns hot in the sullen
    red heart of the East;
Thy whisper is fraught with the laughter of birds and
    the murmur of fountains,
  And the vagabond sons of men throng glad to the joy
    of thy feast.

Harvard Monthly
May 1910

Willamette

O pleasant stream,
Born where the uplands dream
Beneath the summer sky,
Brought forth to give a people life, and die
Forever vanquished in the cosmic strife,
Where the clear current girds the shining fields
There is my heart;
Where in the golden afternoon
The silver trout upstart,
And where the spreading orchard yields
A solemn shade
To elfin folk beneath the harvest moon
For elfin dance arrayed.
Long, long ago
Still did the eerie morn
Pale the dark stream and edge the pines with fire,
Ere yet was born

The star-white city of my birth
And my desire,
The garden-spot of earth.
And through the night
Still came the sound of singing, as you passed
Proudly and strong, to join yourself at last
To the Columbia, against the sea,
Great leader of a hopeless cause eternally.

Pacific Monthly

July 1910

The Charge of the Political Brigade

Twenty votes, thirty votes
Forty votes onward
Into the voting booth
Strode the three hundred
"Forward the Fools' Brigade,
After their votes!" he said
So to the ballot box
Strode the three hundred.

"Forward, O Democrats!
Down with black Derby hats!"
How could the Party know
Someone had blundered?
Their's not to make reply
Their's not to reason why
Their's but to vote - and lie.
Into the voting booth
Strode the three hundred.

Pickets to right of them
Jobs to the left of them
Soreheads in front of them
Shouted and thundered.
Hounded with shot and shell
"Let the Street go to Hell
We'll do the job as well!"
As they collected votes,
Cried the three hundred.

"Charge the Committee then!"
Three hundred stalwart men

Traitors to Nineteen Ten
Broke the class spirit while
All the world wondered.
Swayed by false argument,
Urged to the Polls they went
Scoundrels and ignorant
Worthy three hundred!

Editor's Note: This is a parody of Alfred Lord
Tennyson's "The Charge of the Light Brigade". 1910

        The Wanderer to His Heart's Desire

There you - here I;
Not all the sweetness of your face,
Nor joy of your fair company,
Can bring us to one place.

I think of you -
A picture framed in sombre trees,
Eyes where a gleam of sky breaks through,
Grey days on summer seas.

The Western Wind,
That runs the prairie like a flame,
Bears in his fragrant garments twined
A whisper of your name.

In some far land,
When I desire your comradeship
And the cool frankness of your hand,
The sweetness of your lip.

Then do you send
A blown kiss in the wind's long hair;
And though I sleep at the world's end
Yet will it find me there.

American Magazine

August 1911

The Foundations of a Sky-scraper

Ghastly the pit with thousand-candle flares
Sharp as a sword, - white, cold and merciless.
Bared to the world, the rock's swart nakedness, -
Shadows, and mouths of gloom, like dragon's lairs.
Thunder of drills, stiff spurting plumes of steam, -
Shouts and the dip of cranes, the stench of earth, -
Blinded with sweat, men give a vision birth,
Crawling and dim, men build a dreamer's dream.

Clamor of unknown tongues, and hiss of arc,
Clashing and blending; screech of wheel on wheel, -
Naked, a giant's back, tight-muscled, stark,
Glimpse of mighty shoulder, etched in steel.
And over all, above the highest high,
A phantom of fair towers in the sky.

American Magazine
October 1911

Faery Song

I

Swing, swing, in the faery ring
Wind of the Tree-tops, Dew of the Rose
Where faeries dance with trailing wing
And the elf-horn blows.

II

Soon, soon, the heavy-eyed moon
Drowsily sinks on the Dawn's pole abreast
And stars snuff out on the still lagoon
In the deep o' the breast.

III

Deep, deep, in the rose-heart sleep
Wind of the Prairie, Dew of the Flower
Till the sun goes and the shadows creep
At the faeries' hour.

1911-1912?

Dawn Serenade

I

Now in the East, pale sleeping fairies weave
Of dreams the wan grey gossamer of dawn,
And lay it on your hair -- so fair, so fair
You sleep -- and yet, the shadowy dancers leave,
The swaying phantoms one by one are gone,
The deathless music fades on breathless air.

II

Wake! All the earth is singing to the sky,
Touch with your eyes the tapers of the morn,
Day rises from the arms of Night. Star-spun,
White roses lift against your balcony
Strange flower-fire. On wings of song up-borne,
The swift lark soars to beat against the sun.

1911-1912?

The First Mate

This shapeless canvas slug
You mumble your prayer-book over
Ere heaving it over the rail -
Was, only this morning, a hale
Crisp-haired, brass-bellied sea-rover -
A slave-driving bucko and thug.

What if the thing should rear -
Rise - loosen that charging tongue,
And lash us forrad like scud!
Our blood's afraid of his blood,
We're slaves to that heap of dung -
Yes, even now and here!

Aw, stand up to him, bullies!
They've hid his eyes in a sack -
Spit on him all you please!
His heart has crumbled like cheese,
Limp is his iron back,
His muscles are slack as pullies.

He didn't go like some –
Swept from the poop in a blast,
Knocked on the head with a boom;
His was no warrior's doom,
Fighting his ship to the last –
He died a <u>clean</u> death – from rum!

Him who stood like a tree
In the shock of the spouting tide
The Great Sea loved as a son;
Yet say "Here lieth one – "
Over the place where he died
"Who hated and feared the sea!"

Throttled with cottage and wife,
With a child and a lamp and a stove, –
Stifled and drunken ashore;
Fled to the Sea as a whore,
And out of his restlessness wove
The dream of a landsman's life!

Green elms that rise like fountains –
Plains like a sea without swells –
A windless and desolate spot;
And, 'stead of the (?)
Or the great guns peeling like bells
The mighty quiet of mountains.

      (unfinished poem)

1911-1912?

      The Slave
  (adapted from the French of Heredia)

Thus, naked, frightful, gaunt with loathsome food,
A Slave, – my body still retains the scars, –
I was born free, where, rising toward the stars,
Old honeyed Hybla lifts his mountain hood.
Alas, I left the happy isle! O friend,
If ever, following the swans' Spring flight,
Your galley's course toward Syracuse shall tend,
Seek her who was my love and my delight.
Is it ordained that I shall ever see
Her somber violet eyes, her heavenly smile,

Caught from the sky when all the gods were young?
Be merciful. Go! Seek Cleariste for me,
And tell her to await me yet a while, -
Know her you will, for she is always sad.

American Magazine

February 1912

June in the City

This rock-rummed Northern land is ringed with bloom -
Each night the warm sky hovers soft and low
Above young strolling lovers, - and I know
That on far beaches drives the sea-salt spume.

Oh for a strength of flowering to thrust
Green leaves up through this iron city street!
Brown thrushes in the twilight, and a sweet
Clean wind to sweep the dim stars free from dust!

American Magazine

June 1912

The Wedding Ring

"And what is this you offer me?" quoth Love.
    A girdle of Red Gold.
And "Gold!" sneered Love in scorn
    (Eyes raining lightnings down)
"Gold!
Am I so tinsel-worn
As to be bought and sold
    Like a woman of the town?"

"But why the Ring?" he queried, wondering.
To bind you in the Law.
"Bind <u>me</u>!" cried Love, full loud
    (<u>A</u> flame of wrath his hair)
"Law!
Am I so feeble-bowed,
That you must burn me raw
    With chains to keep me there?"

"Twixt man and maid?" asked Love, incredulous.
Aye, - for mayhap you die.
"Die, I!" ... Love spurned the thing
    (Flushing imperially)
"Die!"
"Nay ... these that use a Ring
To link them in a lie
    Surely deserve not me!"

American Magazine

August 1912

Valkyrs

In valleys moon-hid or far wastes forlorn,
The pipes of battle skirl.
Whirl, battle, whirl!
From the long tables of the feast
Troop the war-maidens. Monstrous shapes and dim,
Black-winged stallions, shed with flame, await;
"To horse!" shrieks Heindall. "In the mystic East,
The thin stars waver and grow pale."
And straight
Up the wide arc of empty sky they spring
Swift galloping:
While on their gleaming mail,
Soft star-fire fades and flickers.

Weep not for those that died.
Full thousand years ago, the shapeless Norns,
In caverned dusk, beat out the fateful runes
On Odin's shield. All lovely April morns,
All golden afternoons summer afternoons.
All joy, all pain,
Are but a stop in the resistless march
Of world on world;
Until the Giants break the rainbow arch,
And all the Gods are into chaos hurled,
And the All-Father is alone again.
O gently lift the warrior-dead, -
Cool hands immaculate, -
Smooth from his brow all suffering and hate,
Crown the fair wounded head
With gnome-wrought circlet of red gold.

Mid whirr of countless wings invisible,
They soar and sweep through pale dawn-glimmering, -
Torn by the talons of the rising gale,
The hurrying clouds are hurled
Across the pallid moon; and o'er the world
The lights die one by one . . .
O what avail
The useless graves upon the hill -
The winding-sheets by mother-fingers spun . . .?
Stark through the wailing of the wind, unbound,
The brazen war-throats burst,
Accurst!
And break the column still,
A flaming rocket-star of sound.

Down the white highway panic hoof-beats thrum,
Wild-horsed, one thunders past
Storm-throated. Villages afar
Wake to a scream above the whistling blast,
"War! War!"
And now they come,
From rose-wreathed farm and quiet hamlet creeping,
Flaring the fight, red-nostriled, helmeted, -
High-hearted Youth,
Thin faces sure led with Truth.
A million dead,
Weary of war, stir in their ageless sleeping . . .

In the high heaven, beyond the utmost gate
That mortal vision bars,
Where summer days unborn
Sleep mid the windy stars, -
Elate
Blares Baldur's silver trumpet-call,
From Odin's court-yard. Up the warriors leap,
In the high-vaulted here-hall;
For somewhere down the weary world asleep,
Far, far below, a vanquished King,
Fear-driven down the world,
Hears faintly in the voices of the gale
A mighty shout where, Orient-impearled,
Valhalla opens wide its gate:
"Hail, hero, Hail!"

In royal state,
Quaff deep the Ever-Living; then alone,
The youngest Valkyr climbs the winding stair
To Odin's empty throne,
Soft comes the sound of revelry

Into the pale and nervous air;
And a thin melody
Is all the shouting battle-song.
On God's far garden-wall the maiden sees,
March up the East dawn's awful blazonries,
All tremulous, the slendor hands of day,
And sails adream the azure deep along;
All wastrels of the night that hide away
At sunrise; every flower and bird and tree,
Each slumbering wee child, -
The fisher's shelter by the sea,
And the lone huntsman in the wild . . .

See! In the youngest Valkyr's eyes,
Swift tears arise -
For in a cottage where the roses creep,
A smiling mother whispers in her sleep.

1912

"This Magazine of Ours"

Cynic

There's pest of politicians - pest
Of every half-cracked whim of Youth;
Each truth is half a lie at best, -
And yet <u>you think you tell the Truth!</u>

Editor

Who knows the Truth? We can but give
White light and wind to every thought
That shakes the world; alone shall live
That part of Truth that's battle-wrought.

Cynic

Men's thoughts are commonplace and mean, -
Wind-vanes that turn and turn again.
You that should be so cold, serene -
Why kneel you in the dust of men?

Editor

Out of the dust of men shall well
All Beauty. Every whim of Youth
Is white-hot Life - And so, to tell
Humbly of Life, - is that not Truth?

American Magazine
July 1912

Eleventh Avenue Racket

There is something terrible
about a hurdy-gurdy,
a gipsy man and woman,
and a monkey in red flannel
with a sign "For Rent" on the door
and the blinds hanging loose
and nobody home.
I never saw this.
I hope to God I never will.

  Whoop-de-doodle-de-doo.
  Hoodle-de-harr-de-hum.
Nobody home? Everybody home.
  Whoop-de-doodle-de-doo.
Mamie Riley married Jimmy Higgins last
  night: Eddie Jones died of whooping
  cough: George Hacks got a job on the
  police force: the Rosenheims bought
  a brass bed: Lena Hart giggled at a
  jackie: a pushcart man called to<u>may</u>-
  toes, to<u>may</u>toes.
Whoop-de-doodle-de-doo.
Hoodle-de-harr-de-hum.
  Nobody home? Everybody home.

1912-1913?

Welsh Song

Oh I sat by a wayside on Cairn-y-brain
To rest my weary feet-o
And a dark-eyed lass came along in the rain
And gave me greeting sweet-o
A slim Welsh lass on Cairn-y-brain
That gave me greeting sweet.

Said I "Will ye sit here beneath my tree;
For the rain is in your hair-o"
So she came and sat on the lap of me
And O but she was fair-o.
And I kissed her lips full tenderly
Nor did she seem to care.

But wae! I felt in my mickle seat
A brogilly pricklin' pain-o
And I leaped full up on my weary feet
And spilled her out in the rain-o
For a red ant-hill had been my seat
On the heights of Cairn-y-brain.

Then I doffed my kilties before the lass
In the braw and gawmy weather
And I rolled about on the dewey grass
An' the bonny purple heather -
O she ran away in the rain, alas!
An' we'll naemore be together!

O the miles are long to my weary feet
And there's many a tempting braeside
But I'd rather lack my bread and meat
Than sit again by the wayside
Oh nevermore will I take my seat
By the bonny Cymric wayside.

1912-1913?

      Sangar

           To Lincoln Stefens

Somewhere I read a strange old rusty tale
Smelling of war; most curiously named
<u>The</u> <u>Mad</u> <u>Recreant</u> <u>Knight</u> <u>of</u> <u>the</u> <u>West</u>.
Once, you have read, the round world brimmed with hate,
Stirred and revolted, flashed unceasingly
Facets of cruel splendor. And the strong
Harried the weak . . .
     Long past, long past, praise God,
In these fair, peaceful, happy days.

  <u>The</u> <u>Tale</u>:

    Eastward the Huns break border,
     Surf on a rotten dyke;
    They have murdered the Eastern Warder
     (His head on a pike).
    "Arm thee, arm thee, my father!
     Swift rides the Goddes-bane,
    And the high nobles gather
     On the plain!"

"O blind world-wrath!" cried Sangar,
  "Greatly I killed in youth;
I dreamed men had done with anger
  Through Goddes truth!"
Smiled the boy then in faint scorn,
  Hard with the battle-thrill;
"Arm thee, loud calls the war-horn
  And shrill!"

He has bowed to the voice stentorian,
  Sick with thought of the grave;
He has called for his battered morion
  And his scarred glaive.
On the boy's helm a glove
  Of the Duke's daughter –
In his eyes splendor of love
  And slaughter.

Hideous the Hun advances
  Like a sea-tide on sand;
Unyielding, the haughty lances
  Make dauntless stand.
And ever amid the clangor,
  Butchering Hun and Hun,
With sorrowful face rides Sangar
  And his son . . .

Broken is the wild invader
  (Sullied, the whole world's fountains);
They have penned the murderous raider
  With his back to the mountains.
Yet though what had been mead
  Is now a bloody lake,
Still drink swords where men bleed,
  Nor slake.

Now leaps one into the press,
  The hell 'twixt front and front –
Sangar, bloody and torn of dress
  (He has borne the brunt).
"Hold!" cries, "Peace! God's peace!
  Heed ye what Christus says –"
And the wild battle gave surcease
  In amaze.

"When will ye cast out hate?
    Brothers - my mad, mad brothers -
Mercy, ere it be too late,
    These are sons of your mothers.
For sake of Him who died on Tree,
    Who of all creatures, loved the least - "
"Blasphemer! God of Battles, He!"
    Cried a priest.

"Peace!" and with his two hands
    Has broken in twain his glaive.
Weaponless, smiling he stands -
    (Coward or brave?)
"Traitor!" howls one rank, "Think ye
    The Hun be our brother?"
And "Fear we to die, craven, think ye?"
    The other.

Then sprang his son to his side -
    His lips with slaver were wet,
For he had felt how men died
    And was lustful yet;
(On his bent helm a glove
    of the Duke's daughter,
In his eyes splendor of love
    And slaughter) -

Shouting, "Father no more of mine -
    Shameful old man - abhorr'd
First traitor of all our line!"
    Up the two-handed sword.
He smote - fell Sangar - and then
    Screaming, red, the boy ran
Straight at the foe, and again
    Hell began . . .

Oh, there was joy in Heaven when Sangar came.
Sweet Mary wept, and bathed and bound his wounds,
And God the Father healed him of despair,
And Jesus gripped his hand, and laughed and
    laughed . . .

Poetry
December 1912

Tamburlaine

A VOICELESS shaking of the air . . .
Then a low shuddering of sound
Vibrant, thunderous, like the profound
Pulsation of great wings. O rare,
In the high-vaulted transept's gloom
Wakes sonant echoing, and the deep
Tone-breakers gather ponderously and leap
From beam to beam, like sullen boom
Of lazy summer thunder. See!
On the bare rock-rimmed Scythian plain
The swarthy shepherd Tamburlaine . . .
Swells the great organ suddenly
Steady, glorious, like a galleon flinging
Leeward the roaring foam - and swift
The soaring organ-voices lift
Terrible as a Crusade singing!
"Tamburlaine! Tamburlaine! Tamburlaine!
Doom of the world's Emperors!
O living Pestilence of Wars,
Thou art God's Scourge, O Tamburlaine!"
Loosed are the shrill, the high pipes' throats,
Joyful the bright, gold trumpets' blare,
Brazen his monstrous armies flare,
Ruthless his red gonfalon floats!
War! Full-throated, the shattering
Great pipes tumultuous give tongue -
Each chord a butchered city sung,
And every note a slaughtered king.
The flame of cities has scorched God's face,
Murder has made a marsh of the world
Purged with destruction - and down-hurled
Rot the world's tyrants . . . Lo! the bass:
"God's lash is bloody, Tamburlaine.
Break, heart die, - Emperor of Kings,
Tool of divine and awful things
Too near to godhead, Tamburlaine!"
Falls like a sea-wind at sundown
The full-toned sonorous battle-chant,
Yet the sound-surf reverberant
Rolls the dim-springing nave adown
Rolls thunderous - subsiding - low -
In a burnt, treeless land where loom
The world's high mountains, lies a tomb -
Vibrant the shuddering tremolo -
A tomb half hid with drifting sand,
Nameless in Samarkand . . .

American Magazine - January 1913

A Hymn to Manhattan

O let some young Timotheus sweep his lyre
Hymning New York. Lo! Every tower and spire
Puts on immortal fire.
This city, which ye scorn
For her rude sprawling limbs, her strength unshorn -
Hands blunt from grasping, Titan-like, at Heaven,
Is a world-wonder, vaulting all the Seven!
Europe? Here's all of Europe in one place;
Beauty unconscious, yes, and even grace.
Rome? Here all that Rome was, and is not;
Here Babylon - and Babylon's forgot.
Golden Byzantium, drunk with pride and sin,
Carthage, that flickered out where we begin . . .
London? A swill of mud in Shakespear's time;
Ten Troys lie tombed in centuries of grime!
Who'd not have lived in Athens at her prime,
Or helped to raise the mighty walls of Rome?
<u>See</u>, <u>blind men</u>! <u>Walls</u> <u>rise</u> <u>all</u> <u>about</u> <u>you</u> <u>here</u> <u>at</u> <u>home</u>!
Who would not hear once more
That oceanic roar
"Ave! Ave Imperator!"
With which an army its Augustus greets?
Hark! <u>There's</u> an <u>army</u> <u>roaring</u> <u>in</u> <u>the</u> <u>streets</u>!
This spawning filth, these monuments uncouth,
Are but her wild, ungovernable youth.
But the skyscrapers, dwarfing earthly things -
Ah, that is how she sings!
Wake to the vision shining in the sun;
Earth's ancient, conquering races rolled in one,
A world beginning - <u>and</u> <u>yet</u> <u>nothing</u> <u>done</u>!

American Magazine
February 1913

Deep-Water Song

The bounding deck beneath me,
    The rocking sky o'erhead,
White, flying spume that whips her boom,
    And all her canvas spread.

Her topmast rakes the zenith,
    Where planets shoal and spawn,
And to her stride God opens wide
    The storm-red gates of dawn!

Then walk her down to Rio,
    Roll her 'cross the line;
China Joe's a-tendin' door
    Down to Number Nine.
Deep they lie in every sea,
    Land's End to the Horn –
For every sailorman that dies
    A sailorman is born.

Along the battered sea-wall,
    Our women in the rain
Full wearily have scanned the sea
    That brings us not again.

Oh, I'll come home, my dearie –
    Aye, one day I'll come home,
With heaped-up hold of Spanish gold
    And opals of spun foam.

Then walk her down to Frisco,
    Lay her for Hong-Kong;
Reeling down the water-front
    Seven hundred strong.
Deep they lie in every sea,
    Land's End to the Horn –
For every sailorman that dies
    A sailorman is born.

Tall, languid palms that glimmer,
    Blossoms beyond belief,
Sea-gods at play in shouting spray
    On sun-splashed coral reef.

O falling star at twilight,
    O questing sail unfurled,
Through unknown seas I follow these
    Down-hill across the world.

<u>Then</u> <u>walk</u> <u>her</u> <u>down</u> <u>to</u> <u>Sydney</u>,
      <u>Through</u> <u>to</u> <u>Singapore</u>;
<u>Dutch</u> <u>Marie</u> <u>and</u> <u>Ysobel</u>
      <u>Waitin'</u> <u>on</u> <u>the</u> <u>shore</u>.
<u>Deep</u> <u>they</u> <u>lie</u> <u>in</u> <u>every</u> <u>sea</u>,
      <u>Land's</u> <u>End</u> <u>to</u> <u>the</u> <u>Horn</u> -
<u>For</u> <u>every</u> <u>sailorman</u> <u>that</u> <u>dies</u>
      <u>A</u> <u>sailorman</u> <u>is</u> <u>born</u>.

Century

March 1913

                        April

    <u>April</u>!
<u>Bird-notes</u> in a gust of rain,
<u>Silver</u> trumpets shivering
<u>Spring's</u> steel armament again -
<u>Hear</u> <u>the</u> <u>world's</u> <u>blood</u> <u>mount</u> <u>and</u> <u>sing</u>
<u>Sweetly</u> <u>on</u> <u>the</u> <u>flowery</u> <u>plain</u>!

    <u>April</u>!
<u>Withers</u> all the grass and dies,
Here the flowers dull and fade -
How shall cities know her guise?
<u>See</u> <u>this</u> <u>new-met</u> man and <u>maid</u>
<u>Tremble</u> <u>at</u> <u>each</u> <u>other's</u> <u>eyes</u>!

American Magazine

April 1913

                , A Song for May

It seems I have not breathed till now,
Nor felt such deep and still delight;
The wind's a cool hand on my brow,
And I am robed in night -
In high and lordly night.

I want not gold nor silken grace,
Nor to be straw to men's desire;
I'd clasp again my mother's face
Before the evening fire -
The warm, transfiguring fire.

I want not love, - alas, I hear
A spurred horse racing on the sand, -
Ah, woe is me! I fear, I fear,
My lover's burning hand -
His hot and eager hand!

American Magazine

May 1913

River Side

On the south side of the hill
Out of the wind
I sat we down to rest.
At my back a lichened wall,
A rough, heaped-up wall of gray boulders, -
(What patient labor of man goes into the gathering of
   stones!)
Under my feet the rusty fields -
Brush of smoke-rose, yellow reeds, dull purple masses
   of trees fretting the pale sky.
A world cleft in irregular blocks of ashen colors
By blundering stone-walls that east block shadows.
Over against we a hill crouched in desolation like a
   lion;
A jade-colored rock upon his breast
Fountained a living spring,
Frozen in monstrous shapes, a row of alabaster gods
Grotesque, with hands upon their knees
Like Hindu idols guarding a king's tomb.
And O, the subtle-toned and bristling marsh
Dead-rose and olive-green, - white shields of ice
   beneath -
Russet and amber and faded lilac, -
Dimmed like breath on a mirror;
Blended and toned as colors seen through a fog, -
Yet under the cold thin light of the wintry day
Fixed, bloodless and dead.
So, gazing upon last year's furrows, and the marks
   of old ploughs,

And the drear scattered houses, feathered with little
    smoke,
And the lean cattle backing to the wind,
And the dim hobbling men stiffly carrying in wood,
And the pale thwarted faces of their women at the
    windows, -
I thought, this is death, - this is lassitude and
    sterility unending, -
Rocks and weeds and back-bowing work have stunted the
    soul of this place,
Faith has the world none, nor future save fruitless,
    monotonous drudgery, -
Stunted souls too weary to aspire, - and deadened
    brains too driven to do battle,
Anemic fields unfertile with much ploughing.

1913?

A Farmer's Woman

I know a patient, nobly-curving hill
That wears a different paleness every hour, -
Copper by sun, grey-velvet through a shower, -
Topaz and mauve, - blue of the heron's quill.
Forever mean-souled ploughmen scar the soil,
And bind, with rambling stony walls, her breast -
Never allow her weary womb to rest,
Nor give a moment's peace for all her toil.

O, if the ploughmen knew what wonders spring
From fields that for a season fallow lie -
Under the healing hand of wind and sky -
Would they not grant her time for flowering!
Her heart is rock. I wonder if her tongue
Knows how to say "I also once was young"?

The Masses

July 1913

Noon

Swirl and pass of listless eyes,
    Thronging up the breathless street;
Clang and **roar** of iron wheels
    In the midday heat.

Nervous noon-tide whistles shrill,
    Stabbing through the sullen air;
Hoarse, defiant, like a voice
    Dauntless in despair.

See! Against the blinding sky,
    High above the steel-shod hoofs,
Moving wisps of coloring
    On the factory roofs.

Waving arms and streaming hair,
    Joyous-leaping, hand in hand,
Sweat-shop girls with lifted face
    Dance a saraband.
Not a tap of rhythmic feet,
    Not a shred of melody,
Lilting thinly on the height,
    Flutters down to me.

Whirling dust of city streets,
    Recklessly they laugh on high;
Tiny motes across the sun
    Dancing in the sky!

Collier's
July 26, 1913

Winter Night

High hangs the hollow, ringing shield of heaven,
Embossed with stars. The thin air wounds like steel,
Stark and resilient as a Spanish blade.
Sharp snaps the rigid lake's mysterious ice,
And the prim, starchy twigs of naked trees
Crackle metallic in an unfelt wind.

A light-poised Damoclean scimitar
The faintly-damascened pale moon. Benumbed
Shrinks the racked earth gripped in the hand of Cold.
O hark! Swift, anvil-ringing iron hoofs
Drum down the boreal interstellar space:
The Blue Knight rides, spurring his snorting stallion
Out of the dark side of the frozen moon -
Eyes crueler than a beryl-sheathed crevasse,
Breath like the chilly fog of polar seas,
Glaciers for armor on his breast and thighs,
A polished Alp for helmet, and for plume
The league-long Northern Lights behind him floating,
Glorious up the sky!

The Blue Knight rides
With his moon-shimmering, star-tipped lance at rest,
Drives at the world - Crash! and the brittle globe
Bursts like a crystal goblet - shivering, falling,
Shivers, splinters bristling, tinkling, jarring,
Jingling in fading dissonance down the void -
Jangling down the unplumbed void forever . . .

American Magazine
January 1914

A Dedication to Max Eastman

There was a man, who, loving quiet beauty best
Yet could not rest.
Attuned to the majestic rhythm of whirling suns,
That chimes and runs
Through happy stillnesses - birth in the dawn, and
    stark
Love in the dark;
The unconquerable semen of the world, that mounts
    and sings
Through endless springs,
And the dumb death-like sleep of the winter-withered
    hill
That warms life still;
There was a man, who, loving quiet beauty best,
Yet could not rest
For the harsh moaning of unhappy humankind,
Fettered and blind -
Too driven to know beauty and too hungry-tired
To be inspired.

From his high, windy-peaceful hill, he stumbled down
Into the town,
With a child's eyes, clear bitterness, and silver
    scorn
Of the outworn
And cruel mastery of life by senile death;
And with his breath
Fanned up the noble fires that smoulder in the breast
Of the oppressed.
What guerdon, to forswear for dust and smoke and this
The high-souled bliss
Of poets in walled gardens, finely growing old,
Serene and cold?
A vision of new splendor in the human scheme -
A god-like scream -
And a new lilt of happy trumpets in the strange
Clangor of Change!

Hillacre Broadside
1916

Two Rooms
60

"Suite number 60 consists of an extra large room on
the quiet side of the building, with private bath and
extra service. The rate is $15 per day."

Hospital Catalogue

There was a bustle in the ward the day he came,
A smell of cold furs, purr of limousines,
A sharp-heeled chauffeur carrying valises
And staggering flunkey feet supporting him.

The nurse was excited. "Who d'you think's in 60?
"Bertram C. Pick, you know, the Ice Trust man.
"My, you just ought to see his overcoat -
"Real sable. And the Mayor sent some orchids . . .
"One of the girls went in to see if he wanted anything,
"And he just opened his eyes and swore at her . . .
"His night nurse is a friend of mine, Belle Stevens
"Her name is; she says he's as democratic
"As if he didn't have ten million dollars . . ."

"Bright's," my doctor told me, looking serious.
"Too much drink, strong cigars - er - no exercise.
"The cares and responsibilities of a great corpora-
     tion . . .
"A big man, splendid advertising for the hospital -
"Not much hope - too bad - a loss to the country . . ."
There were two world-known specialists in attendance -
One cabled for across three thousand sea-miles -
The house-physician and two jealous internes.
They gave out hourly bulletins to the papers,
And three reporters camped out in the waiting-room . . .

The orderly was aglow with reflected greatness.
"All swelled-up and yallow-faced he lays there,
"A short fat man, rolling around and grunting.
"The head-nurse says, 'Would you like a private
     nurse, sir?
"'Thirty dollars a week - 'And he breaks in,
"'Gimme a couple. I don't care what they cost!'
"Like it was nothing. The paper says he's got
"A steam yacht, private car, and he don't know how
     many automobiles;
"A house in New York, and places in Newport and
     Florida . . .
"Well, one thing's sure, he can't take 'em with him
"Where he's going. But if I had 'em, I should worry!"

The last few days his wife and daughter sat
Rustling silks and whispering, outside my door . . .
"Why can't I?" hissed a hard, querulous young voice.
"The Bevins went abroad when Jasper died,
"And nobody thought anything about it -
"I'm sick of staying around here all my life
"Without enough money to do what I please;
"I'm going to travel now and have some fun!"

Toward the end, as he twisted gasping on his bed
In that quiet room, with his special nurses, and
     orderlies,
And all that science can do, to ease his body,
And orchids to ease his soul, and telegrams and cables
From kings, presidents, parliaments, stock-exchanges -
I wondered if his burning kidney reminded him
Of that hot summer, when the fevered slums
Spewed out dead babies, and he made his pile . . .

"Rooms 53 and 54 are furnished and endowed by Mrs.
Bertram C. Pick, in memory of her husband. They can
be had for the minimum rate of $4 per day, payable in
advance".

                         - Hospital Catalogue.

I knew him only by his ludicrous screaming -
Four times a day, three times a night -
Before they punched him with the hypodermic.
"O my God, I can't stand it! O my God, give me
    something!"
And then the nurse came grumbling in
Scolding, "You ought to be ashamed of yourself -"
And the bitter morphine dragged his yelling down
Dissonantly to a groan, a mumble, -
The doctor said,
"A most interesting case.
"An acute cystitis, long neglected,
"Infected bladder, ureters, kidneys - in fact
"The entire superpubic - you wouldn't understand.
"Possibly a year's rest in a warm climate
"Might have cleared up all the symptoms.
"Yes, now there's nothing to be done
"But morphine injections to dull the pain . . .
"How long? O consciousness will probably
"Persist six weeks - and by that time the sedative
"Will be powerless . . . and then two weeks coma . . .
"It is extraordinarily virulent. I've never seen
"Such rapid progress . . . Kill him? Ha, ha.
"Well no, really. It's our duty, you know.
"To preserve life as long as possible - and besides,
"The last stages are particularly interesting . . ."

The nurse said
"Those kind of patients are a bother.
"They make so much noise nobody else can sleep,
"And the whole ward's got to tend to them.
"A man as sick as that ought to have a private nurse;
"Well, if he can't afford it, he oughtn't to be here
"Spending four dollars a day. There's the public ward,
"That's free, and as good a place to die as this . . .
"Yes, a wife. She was here at first,
"Found out how long it would last, and paid
"Five weeks in advance. Said she couldn't stay
"But had to go home and work for the rest
"Before it was due. That's what I call funny!"

The orderly said,
"He puts his finger on the bell
"And keeps it there; and if I don't come he hollers.
"Last time I got mad. 'What in hell' I says
"'Do you think I am? Your private valley?' I says . . .
"When he come here he had on overhalls,
"A brick-layer, I think he was - can't even talk
"Good grammar . . . Say, you ought to see him
    stripped;
"Legs like tooth-picks, and the comicalest thin
    tail . . .
"Say, you know why he don't take no baths?
"Because we're scared he'll go down through the plug-
    hole
"And stop up the pipes - pretty good, eh?"

Well, he staid in 53 - so his wife was working.
And before the dope stopped acting, he was so weak
You could hardly hear his wheezing moan at all,
Although you knew his soul was screaming always . . .
And then even that stopped, and the nurse sighed
Relievedly, "Thank heavens, " she said, "that's
    over . . .
"Did you hear us girls all laughing this morning?
"The new patient in 45 - he's the funniest man
"I overheard talk. The first thing he says to me,
"When I put the thermometer into his mouth, was
"Don't you go off to the movies now!'"

But all I could think of was death in 53
Without love, or battle, or any glorious sudden-
    ness . . .

Unpublished

1916

Love at Sea

Wind smothers the snarling of the great ships,
    And the serene gulls are stronger than turbines;
    Mile upon mile the hiss of a stumbling wave
        breaks unbroken -
Yet stronger is the power of your lips for my lips.

This cool green liquid death shall toss us living
    Higher than high heaven and deeper than sighs -
    But O the abrupt, stiff, sloping, resistless foam
Shall not forbid our taking and our giving!

Life wrenched from its roots - what wretchedness!
    What waving of lost tentacles like blind sea-
        things!
    Even the still ooze beneath is quick and profound -
I am less and more than I was, you are more and less.

I cried upon God last night, and God was not where
        I cried;
    He was slipping and balancing on the thoughtless
        shifting planes of sea.
    Careless and cruel, he will unchain the appalling
        sea-gray engines -
But the speech of your body to my body will not be
    denied!

The Masses
May 1916

Pygmalion

Pygmalion, <u>Pygmalion</u>, <u>Pygmalion</u> -
A mountain meadow loved Pygmalion.
Where a great shining rock like a fallen shield
Lay heavily in tall grass, he rested once.
Long did it hold the pulsing warmth of his body.
And the apple-tree that shaded him, remembered him;
Grass that was new-born trembled under his feet -
Old withered grass felt green beneath his feet -
And the wide view that sank like sleep after pain
Miles over toppling hills to the wide, still river,
Robed itself in opal, golden and haze for him.

While the sun's shadow stood between light and light
He came, paused and was gone. Though never, never
In the world's old contentment had there passed
Before him any human in this place,
Yet lonely were the rock, the tree, the grass.
Longing of the starved heart for a lover gone,
When all is as before, and yet how empty!

White moved his body, crushing the ferns in the valley,
And his happy singing died along far roads;
But loved followed after him - flickered across his
    sleep,
Breathed pride into his walk, power into his hand,
Sweet restlessness into his quiet thought -
Till he who had needed life now needed more;
And so at last he came to the hills again.

<u>Pygmalion</u>, <u>Pygmalion</u>, <u>Pygmalion</u> -
He said in his pride "Thou art wild, and without
    life!"
Never feeling the warm dispersed quiet of earth,
Or the slow stupendous heart-beat that hills have.

<u>Pygmalion</u>, <u>Pygmalion</u>, <u>Pygmalion</u> -
He wrenched the shining rock from the meadow's breast,
And out of it shaped the lovely, almost-breathing
Form of his dream of his love of the world's women.
Slim and white was she, whimsical, full of caprice;
Bright sharp in sunlight, languid in shadow of cloud,
Pale in the dawn, and flushed at the end of day.
Staring, he felt of a sudden the quick, fierce urge
Of the will of the grass, and the rock, and the
    flowering tree;
Knew himself weak and unfulfilled without her -
Knew that he bore his own doom in his breast -
Slave of a stone, unmoving, cold to his touch,
Loving in a stone's way, loving but thrilling never.

In smothering summer silence, pricked with crickets,
Still fell the smiting hammer; happy and loud
Swelled the full-throated song of the adult grass . . .
Full-breasted drooped the tree, heavy with apples . . .
A wind worn lean from leap-frog over the mountains
Spurted the stiff faun-hair of him - whipped desire,
And a bird song "Faint-faint-faint with love-love-
    love!"

Blind he stood, while the great sun blundered down
Through planets strung like beads on careless orbits;
Blind to the view that sank like sleep after love,
Miles over blazoned hills to the brazen river,
Ceaselessly changing, color and form and line,
Pomp, blaze, pageantry new to the world's delight . . .

Hot moist hands on the glittering flanks, and eager
Hands following the chill hips, the icy breasts -
Lithe, radiant, belly to swelling stone -
"Galatea!" - blast of whispering flame his throat -
"Galatea! Galatea!" - his entrails molten fire -
"Galatea! Galatea! Galatea!" - mouth to mouth

Light shadows of driven clouds on a summer lake -
Ripples on still ponds, winds that ruffle and pass -
Happy young grass rising to drink the rain -
So Galatea under his kisses stirred;
Like a white moth alighted breath on her lips,
Like a blue rent in a storm-sky opened her eyes,
Sweetly the new blood leaped and sang in her veins,
Dumbly, blindly her hands, breast, mouth sought
    his . . .

<u>Pygmalion</u>, <u>Pygmalion</u>, <u>Pygmalion</u> -
Rock is she still and her heart is the hill's heart,
Full of all things beside him - full of wind and bees
And the long falling miles and miles of air.
Despair and gnawing are on him, and he knows her
Unattainable who is born of will and hill -
Far-bright as a plunging full-sailed ship that seems
Hull-down to be set immutable in sea . . .

from <u>Tamburlaine</u>, Riverside, Connecticut: Frederick
C. Busch, 1917.

Hospital Notes

Coming Out of Ether

Swish-swish-flash by the spokes of the Wheel of Pain;
Dizzily runs the whining rim.
Way down in the cool dark is slow-revolving sleep,
But I hang heavily writhing in hot chains
High in the crimson stillness of my body,
And the swish-swish of the spokes of the Wheel of Pain.

Clinic

Square white cells, all in a row, with ground-glass
    windows;
Tubes treasuring sacraments of suffering, rubber pipes,
    apparatus;
Walls maculate with old yellow and brown . . .

Out of a mass of human flesh, hairy and dull,
Slim shining steel grows, dripping slow pale thick
    drops,
And regularly, like distant whistles in a fog,
    groaning . . .

Young internes, following the great surgeon like
    chicks a hen,
Crowd in as he pokes, wrenches, and dictates over
    his shoulder,
And hurries on, deaf to the shuddering spirit, rapt
    in a dream of machinery.

Editor's note: John Reed entered Johns Hopkins
Hospital for a kidney infection in November 1916 and
was discharged the following month.

Poetry

August 1917

America 1918

Across the sea my country, my America,
Girt with steel, hard-glittering with power,
As a champion, with great voice trumpeting
High words, "For Liberty. . .Democracy. . ."

Deep within me something stirs, answers -
(My country, my America!)
As if alone in the high and empty night
She called me - my lost one, my first lover
I love no more, love no more, no more . . .
The cloudy shadow of old tenderness,
Illusions of beautiful madness - many deaths
And easy immortality . . .

1

By my free boyhood in the wide West
The powerfull sweet river, fish-wheels, log-rafts,
Ships from behind the sunset, Lascar-manned,
Chinatown, throbbing with mysterious gongs,
The blue thunderous Pacific, blaring sunsets,
Black smoking forests on surf-beaten headlands,
Lost beaches, camp-fires, wail of hunting cougars . . .

By the rolling range, and the flat sun-smitten desert,
Night with coyotes yapping, domed with burst of stars,
The grey herd moving eastward, towering dust,
Ropes whistling in slow coils, hats flapping, yells. . .
By miles of yellow wheat ripping in the Chinook,
Orchards forever endless, deep in blooming,
Green-golden orange-groves and snow-peaks looming
 over . . .
By raw audacious cities sprung from nothing,
Brawling and bragging in their careless youth . . .
I know thee, America!

Fisherman putting out from Astoria in the foggy dawn
 their double-bowed boats,
Lean cow-punchers jogging south from Burns, with faces
 burned leathery and silent,
Stringy old prospectors trudging behind reluctant
 pack-horses, across the Nevada alkali,
Hunters coming out of the brush at night-fall on the
 brink of the Lewis and Clark canyon,
Grunting as they slide off their fifty-pound packs and
 look around for a place to make camp,
Forest rangers standing on a bald peak and sweeping
 the wilderness for smoke,
Big-gloved brakeman walking the top of a swaying freight,
 spanner in hand, biting off a hunk of plug,
Lumbermen with spiked boots and timber-hood, riding
 the broken jam in white water,
Indians on the street-corner in Pocatello, pulling out
 chin-whiskers with a pair of tweezers and a
 pocket-mirror,
Or down on the Siuslaw, squatting behind their summer
 lodges listening to Caruso on a two-hundred
 dollar phonograph,
Loud-roaring Alaska miners, smashing looking-glasses,
 throwing the waiter a five-dollar gold-piece
 for a shot of whiskey and telling him to
 keep the change,
Keepers of dance-halls in construction-camps, bar-
 keeps, prostitutes,
Bums riding the rods, wobblies singing their defiant
 songs, unafraid of death,
Card-sharps and real-estate agents, timber-kings,
 wheat-kings, cattle-kings . . .
I know ye, Americans!

Out of a mass of human flesh, hairy and dull,
Slim shining steel grows, dripping slow pale thick
　　drops,
And regularly, like distant whistles in a fog,
　　groaning . . .

Young internes, following the great surgeon like
　　chicks a hen,
Crowd in as he pokes, wrenches, and dictates over
　　his shoulder,
And hurries on, deaf to the shuddering spirit, rapt
　　in a dream of machinery.

Editor's note: John Reed entered Johns Hopkins
Hospital for a kidney infection in November 1916 and
was discharged the following month.

Poetry

August 1917

America 1918

Across the sea my country, my America,
Girt with steel, hard-glittering with power,
As a champion, with great voice trumpeting
High words, "For Liberty. . .Democracy. . ."

Deep within me something stirs, answers —
(My country, my America!)
As if alone in the high and empty night
She called me — my lost one, my first lover
I love no more, love no more, no more . . .
The cloudy shadow of old tenderness,
Illusions of beautiful madness — many deaths
And easy immortality . . .

1

　　By my free boyhood in the wide West
The powerfull sweet river, fish-wheels, log-rafts,
Ships from behind the sunset, Lascar-manned,
Chinatown, throbbing with mysterious gongs,
The blue thunderous Pacific, blaring sunsets,
Black smoking forests on surf-beaten headlands,
Lost beaches, camp-fires, wail of hunting cougars . . .

By the rolling range, and the flat sun-smitten desert,
Night with coyotes yapping, domed with burst of stars,
The grey herd moving eastward, towering dust,
Ropes whistling in slow coils, hats flapping, yells. . .
By miles of yellow wheat ripping in the Chinook,
Orchards forever endless, deep in blooming,
Green-golden orange-groves and snow-peaks looming
    over . . .
By raw audacious cities sprung from nothing,
Brawling and bragging in their careless youth . . .
I know thee, America!

Fisherman putting out from Astoria in the foggy dawn
        their double-bowed boats,
Lean cow-punchers jogging south from Burns, with faces
        burned leathery and silent,
Stringy old prospectors trudging behind reluctant
        pack-horses, across the Nevada alkali,
Hunters coming out of the brush at night-fall on the
        brink of the Lewis and Clark canyon,
Grunting as they slide off their fifty-pound packs and
        look around for a place to make camp,
Forest rangers standing on a bald peak and sweeping
        the wilderness for smoke,
Big-gloved brakeman walking the top of a swaying freight,
        spanner in hand, biting off a hunk of plug,
Lumbermen with spiked boots and timber-hood, riding
        the broken jam in white water,
Indians on the street-corner in Pocatello, pulling out
        chin-whiskers with a pair of tweezers and a
        pocket-mirror,
Or down on the Siuslaw, squatting behind their summer
        lodges listening to Caruso on a two-hundred
        dollar phonograph,
Loud-roaring Alaska miners, smashing looking-glasses,
        throwing the waiter a five-dollar gold-piece
        for a shot of whiskey and telling him to
        keep the change,
Keepers of dance-halls in construction-camps, bar-
        keeps, prostitutes,
Bums riding the rods, wobblies singing their defiant
        songs, unafraid of death,
Card-sharps and real-estate agents, timber-kings,
        wheat-kings, cattle-kings . . .
I know ye, Americans!

By my bright youth in golden Eastern towns . . .
Harvard. . .pain of growing, ecstasy of unfolding,
Thrill of books, thrill of friendship, hero-worship,
Intoxication of dancing, tempest of great music,
Squandering delight, first consciousness of power. . .
Wild nights in Boston, battles with policemen,
Picking up girls, nights of lurid adventure. . .
Winter swims at L street, breaking the ice
Just for the strong shock on a hard body. . .
And the huge stadium heaving up its thousands
With cadenced roaring cheer or song tremendous
When Harvard scored on Yale. . .By this, by this
I know thee, America!

    By proud New York and its man-piled Matterhorns,
The hard blue sky overhead and the west wind blowing,
Steam-plumes waving from sun-glittering pinnacles,
And deep streets shaking to the million-river -
    Manhattan, zoned with ships, the cruel
    Youngest of all the world's great towns,
    Thy bodice bright with many a jewel,
    Imperially crowned with crowns . . .

    Who that hath known thee but shall burn
    In exile till he come again
    To do thy bitter will, O stern
    Moon of the tides of men!

Soaring Fifth Avenue, Peacock Street, Street of banners
Ever-changing pageant of splendid courtesans,
Fantastic color, sheen of silks and silver, toy-dogs,
Procession of automobiles like jewel-boxes -

Traffic-cop majestical with lifted yellow hand -
Palaces, hotels gigantic, old men in club-windows,
Sweat-shops belching their dun armies at noon-time,
Parades, mile-waves of uniforms flowing up
Bands crashing, between the black still masses of
    people . . .

Broadway, gashing the city like a lava-stream,
Crowned with shower of sparks, as a beaten fire,
Blazing theaters, brazen restaurants, smell of talc,
Movie mansions, hock-shops, imitation diamonds,
Chorus-girls making the rounds of the booking-agencies,
Music-factories blatting from twenty-five pianos,
And all the hectic world of paint and shirt-front . . .

Old Greenwich Village, citadel of amateurs,
Battle-ground of all adolescent Utopias,
Half sham-Bohemia, dear to uptown slummers,
Half sanctuary of the outcast and dissatisfied . . .
Free fellowship of painters, sailors, poets,
Light women, Uranians, tramps and strike-leaders,
Actresses, models, people with aliases or nameless,
Sculptors who run elevators for a living,
Musicians who have to pound pianos in picture-
      houses . . .
Working, dissipating, most of them young, most of
      them poor,
Playing at art, playing at love, playing at rebellion,
In the enchanted borders of the impossible republic. . .

Mysteriously has word of it gone forth
To lonely cabins in the Virginia mountains,
Logging-camps in the Maine woods, desert ranches,
Farms lost in vastnesses of Dakota wheat . . .
Wherever young heart-hungry dreamers of splendor
Can find in all the hard immensity of America
No place to fashion beauty, no companion
To shameless talk of loveliness and love,
Here would they be, elbow on a wooden table at Polly's
Or, borrowing a fiver, over Burgandy at the Brevoort,
Arguing about Life, and Sex, and the Revolution . . .

    The East Side, worlds within a world, chaos of
        nations,
Sink of the nomad races, last and wretchedest
Port of the westward Odyssey of mankind . . .
At dawn vomiting colossal flood of machine-fodder,
At evening sucking back with terrible harsh sound
To beast-like tenements, garish nichelodeons, gin-
      mills.
Kids hanging round the corner saloon, inhaling cheap
      cigarettes,
Leering at the short-skirted girls who two by two go
      giggling by,
Picking their way between crawling babies, over the
      filthy sidewalk . . .
Children at shrill daring games under the hoofs of
      truck-horses -
Gaunt women screaming at them and each other, in
      twanging foreign tongues -
Old men sitting on the crowded stoop in shirt-sleeves,
      smoking an evening pipe,
Glare of push-cart torches ringed with alien faces . . .

In dim Rumanian wine-cellars I am not unwelcome,
Pulsing with hot rhythm of scornful gypsy fiddlers. . .
In Grand Street coffee-rooms, haunt of Yiddish
    philosophers,
Novelists reading aloud a new chapter, collecting a
    dime from each auditor,
Playwrights dramatizing the newspaper headlines, poets
    dumb to deaf America . . .
Fenian saloons, with prominent green flag, and a
    framed bond of the Irish Republic over the bar,
Italian ristorantes, Chianti and spontaneous tenors,
Amenian kitchens hung with Oriental carpets from
    New Jersey,
Where hawk-faced men whisper over thick coffee
    fingering tesbiehs . . .
German bier-stuben, painted with fat mottoes . . .
    French cafes, neat madame at the caisse,
Greek kaffeinias, chop-suey joints with contemptuous
    slant-eyes waiters . . .

    Theatres, Italian marionettes gesticulating Tasso,
Flabby burlesque at Miner's. . .Tomashevsky's Jewish
    coryphees,
Offenbach in Irving Place, winey snap and sparkle,
La Scala Opera Company in Otello at the Verdi -
Ragged costumes, toppling scenery, and voices
    glorious . . .
And the Sicilian Duse, glowing through Giovanitti'
    Tenebri Rossi
Like a volcanic daybreak over the Siberian tundra . . .

Well do I know the Russian brass-shops on Allen Street
The opium-stinking dens of the Cantonese lottery-men
And where the Syrians sell their cool grey water-
    jars . . .

Chathan Square, framed in monstrous kinema-signs and
    the saloons of the damned,
Bowery old-clothes men, stale and sand-floored
    drinking-rooms, spotted with all spittle,
Beef-steak John's, spoken of by sailors in the utter-
    most ports of earth,
Peter Cooper Square in the sick light of before-dawn
Heaped up with homeless men . . . the ten-cent
    lodging-houses
Where shaking wrecks sit dully picking lice around
    the red-hot stove . . .
Stuss-games in sinister back-rooms over on Avenue A,

Dingy law-offices in the shadow of the Tombs, shrines
    of unclean miracles,
The blasted twilight under the hysterical thunder of
    the East River bridges,
And South Street fragrant still with spices of long-
    vanished clipper-ships . . .
Dear and familiar and unforgettable is the city
As the face of my mother . . .

City Hall, never-still whirlpool of the seven millions,
Drowned in the crashing ebb and flow of Brooklyn
    Bridge,
Human cascades from the Elevated, and the Subway
    geysers spouting . . .
The humming newspaper-offices aglitter till the dawn,
Flocks of little newsboys like dusty sparrows
Splashing in the forbidden fountains. . .sleeping
    bums . . .
In the far-flung shadow of legnedary towers . . .
The Battery, sea-wind-cool, at the foot of the sky-
    scraper precipice,
And the sonorous great ships going by, bound for the
    ends of sea,
Squat hurtling ferries, barges stiff with box-cars,
    eagle-crested tugs,
Yellow spray leaping the sea-wall, hoarse gulls
    circling over,
And Liberty lifting gigantic, menacing, out of the
    strife of keels,
Behind it crouching Ellis Island, purgatory of free-
    dom . . .

Exotic Negro-town, upper Amsterdam Avenue,
And its black sensuous easily-happy people, shunned
    of men
The Dark-town Follies, and Europe's ragtime orches-
    tra . . .
Central Park, elegant motors purring along the drive,
Smart cavaliers, perambulators of the upper-classes,
Lovers on benches uneasily spooning, one eye out for
    the cops
And the gasping slums poured out hot summer nights
    to sleep on the meadows . . .
Harlem, New York second-hand and slightly cheaper,
Bronx, post-graduate ghetto, scabby growth of new
    tenements,
Vast green-glowing parks, and the frayed edge of the
    country. . .
Have I omitted you, truck-quaking West Street, dingy

                Death Avenue,
Gracious old Church of the Sea and Land, Inwood, tip of
            Manhattan,
The rag-shops of Minetta Lane, and the yelping swirl of
            the Broad Street Curb,
Macdougal Alley, gilded squalor of fashionable artists,
Coenties Slip, old sea-remembering notch at the back
            of down-town - ?

Nay, across the world, three thoudand miles away,
            without map or guide-book,
Ask me and I will describe them, and their people,
In all weathers, drunk or sober, by sun and moon. . .

I have watched the summer day come up from the top of
            a pier of the Williamsburgh Bridge,
I have slept in a basket of squid at the Fulton Street
            Market,
Talked about God with the old cockney woman who sells
            hot-dogs under the Elevated at South Ferry,
Listen to tales of dago dips in the family parlor of
            the Hell-hole,
And from the top gallery of the Metropolitan heard
            Didur sing "Boris Godounov". . .
I have shot craps with gangsters in the Gas House
            district,
And seen what happens to a green bull on San Juan Hill. .
I can tell you where to hire a gunman to croak a
            squealor,
And where young girls are bought and sold, and how to
            get coke on 125th Street
And what men talk about behind Steve Brodie's, or in
            the private rooms of the Lafayette Baths. . .

Dear and familiar and ever-new to me is the city
As the body of my lover. . .
All sounds - harsh clatter of the Elevated, rumble of
            the subway,
Tapping of policemen's clubs on midnight pavements,
Hand-organs plaintive and monotonous, squawking
            motor-horns,
Gatling crepitation of airy riveters,
Muffled detonations deep down underground,
Flat bawling of newsboys, quick-clamoring ambulance
            gongs,
Deep nervous tooting from the evening harbor,
And the profound shuffling thunder of myriad feet. . .

All smells - smell of sample shoes, second-hand cloth-
            ing,

Dutch bakeries, Sunday delicatessen, kosher cooking,
Smell of damp tons of newspapers along Park Row,
The Subway, smelling like the tomb of Rameses the Great,
The tired odor of infinite human dust-drug-stores,
And the sour slum stench of mean streets. . .

People - rock-eyed brokers gambling with Empires,
Swarthy insolent boot-blacks, cringing push-cart
    peddlers,
The white-capped wop flipping wheat-cakes in the window
    of Childs',
Sallow garment-workers coughing on a park-bench in the
    thin spring sun,
Dully watching the leaping fountain as they eat a
    handful of peanuts for lunch. . .
The steeple-jack swaying infinitesimal at the top of
    the Woolworth flag-pole,
Charity workers driving hard bargains for the degrad-
    ation of the poor,
Worn-out snarling street-car conductors, sentimental
    prize fighters,
White wings scouring the roaring traffic-ways, foul-
    mouthed truck-drivers,
Spanish longshoremen heaving up freight-mountains,
    hollow-eyed silk workers,
Structural steel workers catching hot rivets on high-
    up spidery girders,
Sand-hogs in hissing air-locks under the North River,
    sweating subway muckers, hard-rock men blasting
    beneath Broadway,
Ward-leaders with uptilted cigars, planning mysterious
    underground battles for power,
Raucous soap-boxers in Union Square, preaching the
    everlasting crusade,
Pale half-fed cash-girls in department stores, gaunt
    children making paper-flowers in dim garrets,
Princess stenographers, and manicurists chewing gum
    with a queenly air,
Macs, whore-house madams, street-walkers, touts,
    bouncers, stool-pigeons. . .
All professions, races, temperaments, philosophies,
All history, all possibilities, all romance,
America. . . the world. . . !

The New Masses, October 15, 1935

written: January to March 1918 in Russia

On Returning to the City

Last night I could not sleep for longing -
'Spite the soft wind-rush of the rain, -
The breathless engine-bell's ding-donging,
And the smooth rearing of the train . . .

A flash of lamps, - an echoing thunder, -
The little towns sprang up, - were gone -
Then leaped my soul and I asunder
And the impetuous soul rushed on

To greet these towers where the morning
First kindles from the rim of sea, -
Last pinnacles of Sun's adorning, -
Manhattan: Breath and blood of me!

Manhattan, zoned with ships, - the cruel
Youngest of all the world's great towns, -
Her bodice quick with many a jewel, -
Imperially crowned with crowns, -

Manhattan, threatening above her
The dull gods gaping in the sky -
A Titaness without a lover,
Ringed with a million such as I

Burning to take her passionately -
Burning to buy what is not priced -
Burning to love her hotly, greatly, -
Burning to fill her with a Christ!

The Word! The Word that has no naming, -
Tuned to her mighty pulses' beat, -
That shall awake her senses flaming,
Reckless, and terrible, and sweet

Then shall burst from her lips such singing
As the gods heard at Baldur's birth, -
And all her garments from her flinging,
White, naked, she shall stun the earth!

1918

Proud New York

<u>By</u> <u>proud</u> <u>New</u> <u>York</u> <u>and</u> <u>its</u> <u>man-piled</u> <u>Matterhorns</u>,
<u>The</u> <u>hard</u> <u>blue</u> <u>sky</u> <u>overhead</u> <u>and</u> <u>the</u> <u>west</u> <u>wind</u> <u>blowing</u>,
<u>Steam-plumes</u> <u>waving</u> <u>from</u> <u>the</u> <u>sun-glittering</u> <u>pinnacles</u>,
<u>And</u> <u>deep</u> <u>streets</u> <u>shaking</u> <u>to</u> <u>the</u> <u>million-river</u>:

    Manhattan, zoned with ships, the cruel
        Youngest of all the world's great towns,
    Thy bodice bright with many a jewel,
        Imperially crowned with crowns . . .

    Who that has known thee but shall burn
        In exile till he come again
    To do thy bitter will, O stern
        Moon of the tides of men!

Poetry

April 1919

Fog

Death comes like this, I know -
Snow-soft and gently cold;
Impalpable battalions of thin mist,
Light-quenching and sound-smothering and slow.

Slack as a wind-spilled sail
The spent world flaps in space -
Day's but a grayer night, and the old sun
Up the blind sky goes heavily and pale.
Out of all circumstance
I drift or seem to drift
In a vague vapor-world that clings and veils
Great trees arow like kneeling elephants.

How vast your voice is grown
That was so silver-soft;
Dim dies the candle-glory of your face -
Though we go hand in hand, I am alone.

Now Love and all the warm
Pageant of livingness
Trouble my quiet like forgotten dreams
Of ancient thunder on the hills of storm.

Aforetime I have kissed
The feet of many gods;
But in this empty place, there is no god
Save only I, a naked egoist.

How loud, how terribly
Aflame are lights and sounds!
And yet I know beyond the fog is naught
But lonely bells across gray wastes of sea . . .

Scribner's
August 1919

A Letter to Louise*

Rainy rush of bird-song
Apple-blossom smoke
Thin bells water-falling sound
Wind-rust on the silver pond
Furry starring willow-wand
Wan new grasses walking round
Blue bird in the oak
Woven in my word-song

White and slim my lover
Birch-tree in the shade
Mountain pools her fearless eyes
Innocent all-answering
Were I blinded to the Spring
Happy thrill would in me rise
Smiling half afraid
At the nearness of her

All my weak endeavor
Lay I at her feet
Like a moth from oversea
Let my longing lightly rest
On her flower petal breast
Till the red dawn set me free
To be with my sweet
Ever and forever . . .

Unpublished - 1919

* Editors note: A letter John Reed wrote to his wife,
Louise Bryant from a prison cell in Finland where he
was arrested in transit to Soviet Russia.

Jack Reed - A Memoir

by Max Eastman

I

At the time of his death many people wondered why such a fuss was made about John Reed. "What did he do in Russia that they buried him under the Kremlin wall?" they asked. "You would think he was another Lafayette." Well, he was like Lafayette in this, at any rate- that the Bolsheviks made a hero of him, just as Washington did of Lafayette, not so much because of the services he performed, as because he was a young romantic figure, perfectly shaped and fashioned by nature to become a hero, and they needed a hero of just that kind. They needed a reckless idealist from a foreign land who would come over, like the involuntary gesture of a frowning hemisphere, and cast his lot with theirs.

There was, no doubt, this element in the deification of John Reed. But there was another too, that can only be grasped by those who realize the international theory and feeling of the old Bolsheviks. Reed did do the work of the revolution, at both risk of personal liberty and sacrifice of personal ambition, but he did it in this country, not in Russia. He came home and not only defended the Bolsheviks in articles and speeches all over the country as others did -- though few enough -- but he laid aside all other hopes and rolled up his sleeves and went to work organizing an American Communist party dedicated to the overthrow of the American government and capitalist system, and the institution of a soviet republic on these shores. In order to do that he had to discipline himself, and change himself profoundly. He had to fold his wings and curb his lightnings and be stern. Poets and humorists will know, even if historians do not, that that was fully as high a deed of devotion to the Russian revolution, conceived internationally, as Lafayette's famous "drawing of the sword" was to the revolt of the Thirteen Colonies.

The big difference is that Lafayette was a natural swordsman, and John Reed was not a natural organizer. Lafayette was by character and profession a soldier and man of affairs. Reed was by character

a poet and man of laughter and imagination. He had
to change his nature and mode of life as well as
dedicate his allegiance. In the one-track universe of
the Marxian zealot there is no room for this distinction, and therefore, no room for what I think crucial
in a life story of John Reed -- the fact that the
former change in him was not, and could not have been
permanent. He would never have renounced his
allegiance to the revolution, but he would have come
back to his gay and various self, to those whims and
multicolored interests which were an essential part of
his endowment as a creative writer.

II

Edward J. MacNamara, the tenor and well-known
actor who was a policeman in Paterson during the great
silk strike (and before that an I.W.W.), described
John Reed's jail experience out there. Reproduced with
remote approximation in his own words, it goes like
this:

"'Can't I get into that jail up there,' he says
to the boys, 'without staying more than a day and a
night?'

"'No, you can't do it,' we says, 'If it's overnight, we keep you here in the police station. If
you go up there, you got to stay ten days.'

"'All right,' he says. 'Well, how do I do it?'

"'We'll fix it up for you,' we says. 'Its no
trick at all!' We were herding 'em in like sheep
twenty or thirty in a cell. 'About all you got to do'
we says, 'is stand in line!'"

"So he goes where we tells him and gets his ten
days and moves into the county jail. But he no more
than sits down there than he starts writing articles
in the New York Globe, or the Evening Mail, or somewhere, describing how there's vermin all over the place,
and decayed vegetables and spoiled meat in the soup,
and insects in the salt and pepper boxes. What in hell
would insects be after in the salt and pepper boxes?
There wasn't a word of truth in it, of course, but
there was a lot of sense. The sheriff came down next

morning in a purple rage. 'Where is that writing son of a bitch?' he says. 'Throw him out of here before I break his neck!'"

That is the police story of John Reed's imprisonment and liberation from the Paterson jail. It is far enough, I suppose, from final history, but as a popularized thumbnail sketch, a folk tale of our hero, it has a deep validity.

III

Reed was the most American thing that ever hit Russia since Mark Twain called on the Tsar in the S.S. Quaker City fifty years before. He was too American to be fully understood by that awfully mental and social-conscientious and endlessly instructed "intelligentsia" of theirs. He didn't know what an intelligentsia was. We didn't have them in America. We just tried to be intelligent. He waltzed in there bursting with exuberance and faith in the revolution, zeal to understand it too, found Lenin a laughing man, a man you can make friends with, and clasp hands with, and trust and understand, felt himself perfectly at home in the new proletarian state, and settled down to live there awhile. But life to John Reed meant seeing what could be done; it meant imagination and vast enterprise. I have described in my novel *Venture*, which is partly based on Reed's character, how full he was of gigantic schemes for diverting rivers out of their courses, upsetting the rhythms of the solar system, making barrels of money. Well, he thought up one of these great schemes for the Russian revolution. It was a scheme by which American capital was going to be piped over to Petrograd in floods, and employed all unbeknownst to itself, by some ingenious system of social ducts and by-passages, in building up a great newspaper and explaining everything to everybody and making the world safe for proletarian revolution. I suspect that the scheme was not altogether fantastic -- provided you had perfect faith in the honesty and underlying seriousness of John Reed. But it looked phony to the Russian intelligentsia. It looked either like a disrespectful joke, or a scheme for selling out their revolution -- sidetracking the proletariat when "on the road of fulfillment of its historic mission". Jack thought it would be grand fun to give the proletariat a very ingenious, friendly boost from a most unexpected source along this exciting road -- a joke, yes, but a very timely, meaningful, and helpful joke which all could both enjoy and profit by. That is about how the misunderstanding between John Reed and the Russian intelligentsia shaped up.

In the person of Alex Gumberg the intelligentsia found the prospectus of this enterprise in social and financial engineering in a drawer of Jack's desk. Jack always insisted that Gumberg broke into a locked drawer of his desk to get the papers. Gumberg as vigorously insisted that the papers were lying on the desk. Having heard both stories, I compromise by unlocking the drawer but leaving the papers inside. Anyway, the intelligentsia took the papers straightway off in great seriousness to Lenin, and I don't suppose, when all is said for them that can be, they looked very much like part and parcel of the Historic Mission of the Proletariat. So Lenin, being told by Gumberg, who seriously believed it, that Jack was a frivolous and irresponsible character -- the "playboy" theme again, you see, and any Russian intellectual would have said the same thing about Mark Twain -- revoked Reed's appointment, made by Trotsky a few days before, as Bolshevik consul general at New York.

The way I happened to hear both stories was that I was called on to act as official judge between them. Jack came home in a state of elate wrath at Gumberg, and began denouncing him right and left as a counter-revolutionary. Gumberg, then entering his extraordinary career as contact man between American finance capital and the heads of the Russian revolution, was in a way to be injured by these denunciations far more than he had injured John Reed. Quiet-spoken, imperturbable, secretive, a natural-born mystery man -- ape-like in aspect, at first contact sinister, and afterward inspiring trust -- Gumberg had, as secretary to Raymond Robbins and the American Red Cross, done yeoman's service for Lenin and Trotsky during the revolution. He did yeoman's service afterwards in Wall Street for the Soviet government. His more comely brother, Zorin, was a consecrated party Bolshevik -- one of those who held out against Stalin's usurpation, and spent most of his time in prison. Alex, however, was not a Bolshevik -- not, in my opinion, a revolutionist. However, he was certainly not a counter-revolutionist, and only a man as honest as a compass could have played the subtle role he did for twelve or fifteen years after the Bolsheviks seized power.

It is one of the customs of the Russian revolutionary movement, when an imputation of disloyalty is made, for both sides to present their case to some trusted leader of sufficient prominence so that his decision, publicly announced, will settle the question. I had never heard of this custom, and moreover never thought of myself as a leader, and when Gumberg approached me with a view to my holding court between him and John Reed, and rendering such a decision, I did not understand what he was after. His approach, perhaps, was diplomatic, or diffident, but I thought it was roundabout and unexplicit and mysterious. Being embarrassed myself, and as always in contact with a stranger mainly concerned to get away, I did not put any straight question: What do you want me to do? I merely said yes and yes, and made up my own mind, or what there was of it present, that the thing to do was to bring him and Reed together, and, in the American fashion, get them to shake hands and "call it off."

To this no preliminaries seemed necessary, and I was for calling Reed up. But no -- I must first dine with Gumberg and Raymond Robbins at the Brevoort Hotel, and hear all about their work in Russia, during the revolution! Although astonished, I was delighted to do that. Robbins brought a whole brief case full of correspondence with Lenin and Trotsky and the other Bolsheviks, showing the trust they had placed in him. He had, in fact, played the part of unofficial American ambassador to the new government, the patrician ambassador Francis having disdained to soil his palm against that of a criminal like Lenin. And he assured me that all this would have been impossible, which was pretty obvious, without the loyal help of his Russian secretary Gumberg. I greatly enjoyed meeting Robbins, and hearing all about his sympathy and faith in the Bolsheviks. He was then keeping discreetly quiet about it before the public. We had, in fact, published a cartoon by Art Young, showing him hiding in a tree trunk, and a boy lighting a smudge under the tree: "Will Mr. Raymond Robbins please come out?" I also enjoyed the dinner at the Brevoort -- a place that had always pleased my pseudo-Bohemian fancy but stood above my Bohemian means. But I still did not really understand what this was all about, or what I was supposed to do.

Realizing that I had to do something, however, I made a date with Gumberg and invited Reed to my office at the same time. Gumberg got there first, and we were making conversation -- I very haltingly, for this man of mystery still bewildered me -- when Jack came in. As I remember it, I said:

"Jack, Gumberg wants to have a talk with you."

"Talk!" he said. "Why talk to that counter-revolutionary son of a bitch?"

He hitched up his pants, gave himself a scratch under the arm, looked at me with a gentle, perhaps a slightly shamefaced smile, and walked out of the room.

I shrugged my shoulders. "Well -- I don't see what more I can do!"

And Gumberg went away.

Twelve years later I heard from Floyd Dell that Gumberg thought I was no good because I had refused to "render a decision" between him and John Reed. It was the first inkling I had of what the nature of the whole proceeding had been.

Although Reed's wrath against Gumberg was so implacable, the incident itself did not bother him much or long. At least, so Louise Bryant told me. He was too free of small vanity, and too close friends with Lenin and Trotsky, to let that grow into anything momentous. But it must have given him a hearty shock, and it serves well as a symbol of something that I think did happen to John Reed in contact with those adeptly revolutionary Russians. It put a question to him. It challenged him, as they did, to prove that he was, with all his wit and poetry and reckless jocularity, and what we may call in the best sense "Americanism", loyal and to be trusted in a fight -- a thing that he himself had never thought of questioning. It taught him, as a not dissimilar entanglement teaches Jo Hancock in my novel, that to go adventuring after "reality" in this day brings you inexorably up to the edge of an absolute choice. For "reality" in its most momentous aspect is class struggle. And class struggle is something you don't monkey with, and straddle, and try to dance round on both sides of the way you do round a buzz saw.

I do not mean that intellectually John Reed had not grasped this before. He had. And so had Louise Bryant, who was a *Masses* girl long before John Reed ever met her, known and beloved in our office because her letters of enthusiasm were followed up, as few such letters are, with regularly recurring literal handfuls of subscriptions. *The Masses* brought John Reed and Louise Bryant together, and its policy of revolutionary class struggle for socialism was the trysting place of their minds. *The Masses* itself, however, was a too laughing and singing institution to convince a Russian Bolshevik offhand that it had really taken to heart the Historic Mission of the Proletariat. And John Reed had come to *The Masses* from the evangelical and rebel, not the proletarian and revolutionary side. He represented the Bohemian-anarchist ingredient in that extraordinary amalgam of young rebelliousness, the *Masses* staff. He had, therefore, even more than men like Art Young or John Sloan would have, to prove himself adult and serious about what he had been saying. In the circle of those interested, his relation to the struggle for socialism was not unlike that of Byron to the struggle for national liberty. He was a rebel wit and poet, but caught in by the fame and timeliness of his jests and music to the life of action, and compelled to try to make good as an organizer. And like Byron, at some cost to his temperament and to the literature of his country, he did make good.

IV

I remember one evening after dinner on my porch under the osage-orange tree, Louise and Jack and Florence and I arguing over the coffee cups, and my exclaiming:

"Jack, the trouble with you is you're getting too damned adult!"

And I remember his vast amusement -- it being somewhat a reversal of our previous roles -- and how after that, he would ironically apologize when introducing some serious topic of discussion: "if you will pardon my bringing this up in the presence of children . . ."

I may be influenced in my opinion that this change in Reed's temper was not permanent by the fact that I did not want it to be. Although I make my bow to heroism entailed, I never quite reconciled myself to it. It seemed to me that something more unique than faithful work and courage was sadly getting lost. I feel the same way about Robert Minor's turning himself from a great and flame-communicating cartoonist into a little and second-rate politician in the name of consecration to a cause. I think the primitive indolence of all human flesh before the steep task of forthright creation has usually a larger place among the real causes of such a change, if they could be dug up, than the alleged consecration. In Jack's case I used to question whether it was his removed kidney or the Russian Bolshevik religion which reduced him from his joyfulness and made a rather stern-mouthed earnest saint of him. I still do question it. But I have often noticed that people who experience conversion to a religion -- erect within themselves, that is, a One-and-Only to which all other interests and passions meekly bow down -- and call this "inward bliss", or "spiritual contentment," are often outwardly a little grim and sad. It may have been this that happened to John Reed in Russia.

At any rate, I believe that this change from color and metaphor and laughter to narrowly practical information and statistics -- from a joking poet to a sober saint of practicality -- was but one phase in the development of a rich and varied temperament. And I remember things to prove it. I have described elsewhere how we met on Greenwich Avenue one sunny, balmy, lazy morning under the shadow of that towering red jail, which, whether you remember it is a jail or think it is only a clock tower, decides what party you belong to. I asked him how some part of his political work was going.

"It's all right," he said. "It's going all right . . . You know this class struggle plays hell with your poetry!"

It stuck in my mind, as things always and only do, because of its relation to a system of ideas. It was Jack Reed's testimony on the subject of Art and the Life of Action, a subject which has troubled me, and engaged my best efforts to solve it, either in thought or practice, all my life long. And it was testimony to the effect that he too had not solved it. He was not through. He was not settled. He was doing a job because things had so shaped themselves that it was up to him to do it. So I interpreted his words.

I remember another meeting, and how different, in the middle of Sheridan Square, where just two or three doors from my rooms he wrote Ten Days That Shook the World -- wrote it in another ten days and ten nights or little more. He was gaunt, unshaven, greasy-skinned, a stark sleepless half-crazy look on his slightly potatolike face -- had just come down after a night's work for a cup of coffee.

"Max, don't tell anybody where I am. I'm writing the Russian revolution in a book. I've got all the placards and papers up there in a little room and a Russian dictionary, and I'm working all day and all night. I haven't shut my eyes for thirty-six hours. I'll finish the whole thing in two weeks. And I've got the name for it too -- Ten Days That Shook the World. Good-by, I've got to get some coffee. Don't for God's sake tell anybody where I am!"

Do you wonder I emphasize his brains? Not so many feats can be found in American literature to surpass what he did there in those two or three weeks in that little room with those piled-up papers, in a half-known tongue, piled clear up to the ceiling, and a small dog-eared dictionary, and a memory, and a determination to get it right, and a gorgeous imagination to paint it with when he got it. But what I wanted to comment on now was the unqualified, concentrated joy in his mad eyes that morning. He was doing what he was made to do, writing a great book. And he had a name for it too -- Ten Days That Shook the World!

In short, although John Reed made heroic sacrifices for the revolution, I do not think his fundamental philosophy, or wish of life-philosophy is so often our grandiose name for a wish -- had changed. It was long after that that Louise told me about the terms of their companionship, and she told of it as a thing that lasted to the end. I think that Reed's consecration to the revolution was still a subordinate though integral part of his prior will and ideal -- easy for light nuts to satirize, but old as organic evolution -- the will to "live life". Which meant to live it in freedom and stark reality and immense honesty.

This does not mean that Reed was a fair-weather friend of the revolution. Anything but that. Another of my vivid memories of him -- vivid because he was confiding to me a thing he would have, I think to no one else except Louise -- was the bewilderment with which he quoted something Louis Fraina said to him. It was at the height of their joint campaign to "win the party for revolutionary socialism," and Fraina was living with him at his house in Croton. They had been expressing their certain and excited confidence of victory, and Fraina, to round off the mood of it, remarked: "And if this does fail, why then I'll be ready to turn gentleman."

It seemed to me as though Jack were asking me whether, after all, this revolution business was the real thing or a game that you play.

"I don't think a real revolutionist would say a thing like that, do you?" he said.

It forms a comment on Julian Street's opinion, and the opinion of so many philistines, that to Jack Reed all life was a game to play.

No, Jack Reed's moral integrity, his faithfulness in great matters, was absolute. It is significant that within a week or two after his consulship was withdrawn on grounds of irresponsibility, he was for coming all the way back to America solely in order to stand trial for sedition with us, his colleagues on The Masses, and no less responsible a Bolshevik than Trotsky was trying to persuade him that such an act was quixotic. He was *too* responsible -- that was Trotsky's view, and a view characteristic of Russian Bolsheviks. They neither understood Reed's abandoned spirit of humor and adventure, nor the harsh standard of personal integrity, like Mark Twain's that underlay it.

Anyone who did understand them, and who knew John Reed, could have predicted that where the Bolsheviks abandoned fundamental reality and truth-speaking, and the impetuous honesty that he loved in Lenin, he would abandon the Bolsheviks. He hated priests; he could not endure the smell of the casuist. He hated hypocrisy and jesuitry, and the smug complacense of those who think they represent the purposes of the universe.

He hated deception. He was incapable of it in public or in private life. To Louise Bryant his candor about his impetuous feelings and experiences of love was an earthquake shock -- a shock which she stood up to in the long run with nobility and generosity. "Nobody I love", he wrote to her in their early quarrel, "has ever been able to let me express myself fully, freely and trust that expression". Well, she did let him. She stood sufficiently upon her own feet to become the mate of an impressionable and absolutely forthright man, without lies and without any dissimulation between them.

When Louise arrived in Moscow in the summer of 1920, Jack had to tell her that he had been loving a Russian girl. He was not very much in love; it needn't break their relation. And it didn't. He had also to tell her that he was resigning in bitter disillusion from the executive committee of the Communist International. In both these harsh blows of fortune, to Louise's sensitivity, the same fact was in the foreground. Jack Reed's boldness about being real, his absolute, proud, and intolerant honesty. That is what brought him into conflict with Zinoviev and Radek, and to some extent with the whole ethical philosophy and working morale of Bolshevism. To what extent this latter, I do not know, and I suppose nobody ever will. But his close political and personal friendship with Angelica Balabanoff at this time is of prime significance. The fact that he inscribed a picture for her: "To the best revolutionist I have known in Russia," speaks volumes to those who know her emotional nature and her intellectual position. It speaks volumes to all those who want to know the truth about John Reed's last days, no matter what it is.

THE CONTRIBUTORS

Max Eastman - 1884-1969, the noted essayist, poet, philosopher, critic, translator, memoirist, Mr. Eastman was the author of over 30 books. He was the editor of The Masses and later of Liberator. Author of Enjoyment of Poetry, The Literary Mind, Artists in Uniform, Marxism, Is It Science?, and Enjoyment of Laughter. His memoirs include Enjoyment of Living, Great Companions and Love and Revolution. His poetry was collected in Poems of Five Decades.

Granville Hicks - 1901-1982, the prominent literary critic, book reviewer and novelist, Mr. Hicks was perhaps best known for his review columns in The New Leader (1949-1958) and the Saturday Review (1958-1969). He wrote the authorized biography of John Reed in 1936. His three novels are Only One Storm, Behold Trouble, and There Was a Man in Our Town. His study of life in a small town is generally regarded as a classic: Small Town. Mr. Hicks's literary studies include The Great Tradition, Figures of Transition, and Literary Horizons. His autobiography appeared in 1965 as Part of the Truth.

Jack Alan Robbins - born 1944, received a Ph.D. in political science from Fordham University, with a doctoral dissertation on the Marxist philosophy of Maurice Merleau-Ponty. He has written The Birth of American Trotskyism 1927-1929. He assisted Granville Hicks in editing Literary Horizons. He has also edited Granville Hicks in the 'New Masses'and James T. Farrel: Literary Essays. A previous edition of The Complete Poetry of John Reed was privately printed in 1972. Presently Mr. Robbins is writing a memoir of Granville Hicks and lecturing on American writing and art in the period 1880 to 1916.

Acknowledgements

The compilation of John Reed poems into a single volume involved many people. The editor owes a great debt to the ideas, criticism and encouragement of Granville Hicks and Max Eastman. Carolyn Jakeman of Harvard's Houghton Library helped in making the John Reed Collection housed there available to the editor. Cynthia Angelides helped in preparing copies of Reed's poems in his own handwriting. The staff of Harvard Library facilitated the compilation in several ways and was most courteous to the editor on several trips to Harvard. Corliss Lamont of Harvard's John Reed Committee encouraged the publication of the poetry.

Houghton Library at Harvard granted the editor permission to include those poems of Reed's that were in the John Reed Collection.

My wife, Margaret, typed nearly all of the manuscript in its present uniform composition, correcting and improving upon the original 1972 private printing.

My parents always encouraged my scholarly pursuits. Deserving full gratitude is my wife, Margaret, an editorial critic of ability, who sustains me.